Faith

OF OUR
FOUNDING
FATHER

Other Books by Janice T. Connell

Queen of the Cosmos
The Visions of the Children
Triumph of the Immaculate Heart
Angel Power
Meetings with Mary
Praying with Mary
Prayer Power
Queen of Angels

Faith

OF OUR

FOUNDING

FATHER

THE SPIRITUAL JOURNEY OF

George Washington

JANICE CONNELL

Hatherleigh Press

New York

Faith of Our Founding Father
The Spiritual Journey of George Washington

Janice T. Connell

Hatherleigh Press
5-22 46th Avenue
Long Island City, NY 11101
1-800-528-2550
www.hatherleighpress.com

Library of Congress Cataloging-in-Publication Data

Connell, Janice T.
  Faith of our founding father : the spiritual journey of George Washington / Janice T. Connell.
    p. cm.
  ISBN 1-57826-156-2 (alk. paper)
 1. Washington, George, 1732-1799--Religion. 2. Washington, George, 1732-1799--Philosophy. 3. Presidents--United States--Biography. I. Title.
E312.17.C66 2003
973.4'1'092--dc22

                                              2003018234

All Hatherleigh Press titles are available for special promotions and premiums. For more information, please contact the manager of our Special Sales department.

Cover & interior design by Tai Blanche

Printed in Canada on acid-free paper
10 9 8 7 6 5 4 3 2

Dedication

*T*his book is dedicated to George Washington, and all brave ones, living, deceased, yet to be born, who in any way lend their hearts, skills, strength, and prayers to protect and defend the ideals of the United States of America. May such sacrifice bring upon the earth a holy, peaceful City of God for all.

* * *

There are no coincidences.
It is not by accident that you have this book.

Table of Contents

Cover Image by Arnold Friberg

Foreword

"[I]t is a point conceded that America, under an effi-
cient government, will be the most favorable Country
of any in the world for persons of industry and fru-
gality, possessed of a moderate capital, to inhabit. It
is also believed, that it will not be less advantageous
to the happiness of the lowest class of people because
of the equal distribution of property, the great pleni-
tude of unoccupied lands, and the facility of
procuring the means of substance"[1]
—George Washington

George Washington has much to teach the world today. Three significant realities in his life propelled him to immortality. First, he was born into rather ordinary circumstances. Secondly, he used the opportunities life presented him to feed the hungry, give drink to the thirsty, clothe and shelter the needy, care for the imprisoned, visit the sick, bury the dead, admonish, instruct, counsel, forgive and pray for others. Thirdly, and undoubtedly the most significant, he never allowed success or failure to corrupt him.

George Washington's deeds are his greatest legacy. As you examine the evidence in this small book, treasure the stories that allow Washington's character to shine through the prism of time. You will find that for Washington patriotism meant union with God through loving deeds for humanity. After you weigh the enclosed expert testimony and savor personal examples of Washington's choices in the framework of his life, take the next step. Make a decision. Go forth and use this information. There are no lost opportunities for true patriots.

Chronology

February 22, 1732: Birth of George Washington in British colony of Virginia

1752: Appointed Major of Virginia Militia

1753: Military duty in Ohio Valley, Pennsylvania

1754-1763: French and Indian War

1754: Washington acts as Aide to British General Edward Braddock at battle for Fort Du Quesne

1755–1758: Washington serves as Commander in Chief of Virginia Military forces

1758-1775: Member of Virginia House of Burgess

January 6, 1759: Wedding of George Washington and Martha Dandridge Custis

1765: British Parliament passes the Stamp Act

1773: December "Boston Tea Party"

1774: Washington attends first Continental Congress

1775: Washington elected General and Commander in Chief of the Continental Forces

July 4, 1776: Declaration of Independence

Winter 1777-1778: Valley Forge

October, 1781: Defeat of British General Charles Cornwallis at Yorktown, Virginia

1787: General George Washington elected President of the Constitutional Convention, in Philadelphia

June, 1788: United States Constitution ratified

February 4, 1789: George Washington unanimously elected first President of the United States

February 13, 1793: Washington reelected President for second term

1797: Washington retires to Mount Vernon

December 14, 1799: George Washington dies at Mount Vernon

Introduction

"My first wish is to see this plague to mankind,
war, banished from the earth."
—George Washington

*I*n the unprovoked attack upon America on September 11, 2001, thousands were cremated alive at the World Trade Center in New York, at the Pentagon in Washington, DC., and in the fields of Western Pennsylvania. Ordinary people of every race, nationality, educational and economic background, simply engaged in their daily duties, died in explosions causing heats that approached 2000 degrees. The devastation was so great that those still living under the rubble may have envied the dead.[2] No one can ever measure such suffering.

American History is a comfort to contemporary Americans in their hour of trial, for it teaches that God brings good out of evil. His mercy is greater than all His works.[3] George Washington believed the Gates of Paradise are wide and the Blood of the Lamb has obtained entry for all redeemed children of the Father.[4]

He knew well that every man rises and falls on the choices he makes every moment. Like Abraham and Moses, Washington had pleaded with God, especially at Valley Forge.[5] Throughout his life, Washington appealed to the God of mercy with loud cries.

Washington was not a stranger to sorrow, cold, hunger, persecution, violence or terrorism. George Washington's great accomplishment was to face misfortune and conquer it; he achieved victory by discipline, commitment, prayer and the graced ability to bend his will under the yoke of Divine Providence. He was a stoic who triumphed over suffering with ascetic heroism.

When he was twenty-two years old, Washington was commissioned a Captain by Governor Robert Dinwiddie of Virginia and dispatched to Fort Du Quesne (now Pittsburgh, Pennsylvania) with about 140 officers and men to protect the western lands of the English crown.[6] Young Washington achieved a small victory at Jumonville in the spring of 1754, but not without cost to the sensitivities of his soul. He reported a seminal war incident involving his Indian guides in these words:

"...5 or 6 Indians had chosen to knock the poor, unhappy, wounded [French prisoners of war] in the head, and bereiv'd them of their scalps."[7]

That would not happen again under his watch.

As a young surveyor and youthful military leader in the Ohio Valley, Washington witnessed the terrorism unleashed upon American colonists who "…might well be exposed to the tortures and killings in which the Indians habitually indulged themselves…"[8] He wrote of his personal experience on the frontier:

> " …[F]ive hundred Indians have it more in their power to annoy the inhabitants, than ten times their number of regulars. For besides the advantageous way they have of fighting in the woods, their cunning and craft are not to be equaled, neither their activity and indefatigable sufferings. They prowl about like wolves, and, like them, do their mischief by stealth. They depend upon their dexterity in hunting and upon the cattle of the inhabitants for provisions."[9]

He wrote from the frontier to his superior, Governor Dinwiddie of Virginia, on April 22, 1756:

"The supplicating tears of the women, and moving petitions from the men, melt me into such deadly sorrow, that I solemnly declare, if I know my own mind, I could offer myself a willing sacrifice to the butchering enemy, provided that would contribute to the people's ease." [10]

Washington was a man of great prayer. Shortly before the Declaration of Independence became a reality, the realistic Washington wrote to John Adams on April 15, 1776:

"We have nothing, my Dear Sir, to depend upon but the protection of a kind Providence and unanimity among ourselves." [11]

Divine Providence heard their prayers. Liberty steeped in just law came to life in America, but at a price each subsequent generation of Americans is called upon to honor.

Against insurmountable odds, George Washington courageously led America into the merciful light of freedom. During his lifetime, Washington's faith in the goodness of Divine Providence and the sibling relationship of all the earth's people ignited a fire that warmed the hearts of Native Americans, colonists and

Europeans, rapidly spreading to the entire world. Washington's dream was that people of every race, culture and religion bloom side by side in America as gently as spring breezes nurture flowers and trees and seas and deserts. Washington believed that America, the great land of opportunity, was to play a unique spiritual role in the history of the human race.

George Washington is America's Founding Father whose personal faith in the mercy of Jesus Christ carved out for all to see the American paradigm of liberty steeped in just law. Washington did not act alone. His accomplishments and writings disclose that Providence was in him, around him and always with him.

This small, abbreviated narrative of certain segments of George Washington's life is offered as a resource for those everywhere who seek peace among nations, prosperity, and global fellowship rooted in virtue. May it illumine more brightly the living spirit of American liberty that is available to people of sincere good will everywhere.

The world is at a crossroads. The truth is that the United States is one nation under God, with liberty and justice for all. America's system of government is the child of wisdom and the ward of vigilance. George Washington's faith in God's mercy offers a highly test-

ed opportunity for all people to work together to preserve not only America the Beautiful, but the entire
earth.

The legacy of our Founding Father George
Washington brings forth light from Heaven's Throne
for these times.

PART ONE

PART ONE

CHAPTER ONE

Washington's Early Years

"Without virtue and without integrity the finest talents and the most brilliant accomplishments can never gain the respect or conciliate the esteem of the truly valuable part of mankind."[12]
—George Washington

*G*eorge Washington's forebears were among the early settlers of Virginia; they descended from an English shipmaster, John Washington, who emigrated to Virginia about 1658. John had left England to escape shame and the resulting financial hardship that flowed from religious persecution. His goal was to seek peaceful prosperity in commerce.

John Washington's father had been an ordained Puritan Minister, the Reverend Lawrence Washington of Purleigh, England. Fellow Puritans in England had arbitrarily deprived him of his livelihood, condemning him for practicing Anglican Catholicism. His congregation accused him of "drunkenness" because he continued to say Mass at a time when such practices were not appreciated.[13] Though history is silent about the surrounding details of Reverend Washington's life, the shame of the punishment wrought upon the family was intolerable for young John and he fled to Virginia to escape the social and financial harshness that flowed from its bitterness.

Youthful John Washington found Virginia's soil fertile, and bountiful. The climate was mild and the land was beautiful. Farming was healthful and profitable for him. Before long his discipline and industriousness placed him among Virginia's landed gentility. His posterity would rank among the first families in the colony.

Religious freedom paired with financial opportunity gave John Washington powerful incentives to hold fast to God's ways. Because of his influence, the manners and culture of the Washington family in Virginia remained rooted in an English Puritanism steeped in Anglican Catholicism. The Washingtons, along with others similarly situated in Virginia, did not repudiate the Thirty-nine Articles of Religion of the Anglican faith. However, they did away with the hierarchical strata of clergy, above the rank of parish priest. They also discarded all set prayers, including the Book of Common Prayer.[14] Anglicanism attempted to fuse the best of ancient Christianity with the sensitivities of English desires. Puritanism, however, as practiced by Washington's forbears in Virginia, was a reaction to the frivolity, extravagance and moral corruption that pervaded the English Court, clergy and the upper classes.[15]

Washington's ancestors were among those who strongly believed "life is empty without religion….[T]he tree of knowledge is barren unless rooted in love….[L]earning purchased at the expense of living is a sorry bargain." [16] There was ample time for Bible study in most Virginia family homes. The Washington family library contained theology books that chronicled God's temporal as well as spiritual rewards and punishments for behavior and each subsequent generation studied these works.

George Washington, born on February 22, 1732, was the eldest of six children of Augustine Washington and his second wife, Mary Ball. An orphan when she married George's widower father, she was of moderate height, rounded figure and pleasant voice.[17] She would be a challenge to her son during her entire life. Young George learned from the cradle that the Bible was the source for his spiritual, political and financial life. There were strict laws against breaking the Sabbath, contempt of the Bible, disrespect for its teachings, and speaking against ordained ministers. Idleness, betting, drunkenness and intemperance in attire were forbidden.

Washington's father worked hard to support his large family. He directed a plantation, looked after his other farms and supervised an iron furnace he owned thirty miles distant from his residence. He was no stranger to manual labor and was often away from home attending to his business interests.

Before George was three years old, his half-sister Jane died. When George was six, Lawrence, his twenty-year-old half-brother, who had been studying at Appleby, his father's school in England, returned to Virginia. Elegant, filled with charm, grace and manners, Lawrence would always remain George's hero. Augustine, busy with many occupations, entrusted Lawrence with partial management of the plantation in order to train him in agriculture.

George thrived under the tutelage of his elder brother whom he greatly admired. On June 17, 1740, Governor William Gooch of Virginia commissioned Lawrence one of four military leaders for Virginia, insuring that he would see the forts of Cartagena, hear war cannons and watch battles. George delighted in

Lawrence's cultured manners, military skills and adventurous tales.

Tragedy struck when George was eleven. His father died suddenly, leaving the financial position of his widow and children ambiguous. Lawrence probated his father's will: the estate included more than ten thousand acres, at least forty-nine slaves and an interest in the iron furnace. Young George inherited some real estate and ten slaves. However, his father had directed that the estates of his children by Mary Ball remain in their mother's guardianship during their minority. Thus George's inheritance was not valuable and this fact would require George to acquire keen business skills and develop extraordinary qualities of leadership.

Washington was formed not only by life's experiences, but significantly by education. He who would match wits with the most erudite of men, possessing the finest education of the times, had only a school boy's formal education.

But Washington accomplished his lessons perfectly. In 1745, when George was thirteen years old, he transcribed *The Rules of Civility* in colonial shorthand in his school workbook.[18] These *Rules of Civility* were taught to Washington during his first year of study with Reverend James Marye, a French Jesuit turned

Anglican priest and rector of St. George's Church in Fredericksburg.[19] Reverend Marye also taught Washington mathematics, Latin and deportment. Washington was required to learn the *Rules of Civility* by heart. They were the code of civil, social and cultural behavior for respectable gentlemen of his times.

The history of those *Rules of Civility and Decent Behavior in Company and Conversation* dates from the 1590's. French Jesuit priests distilled these spiritual exercises of their Spanish founder, Ignatius of Loyola, and incorporated them with rules of deportment for European nobility known as **"110 Rules for Young Gentlemen."**[20] Washington's handwritten copy of these Rules in his personal notebook is now in the Library of Congress.[21]

The *Rules of Civility* that governed Washington's code of behavior convey an Ignatian discipline that forms the spiritual man. The **110 Rules for Young Gentlemen** allow their adherents exquisite awareness that man is God's servant, on earth to honor his fellow man as he would like to be honored in everyday life, living not for self, but for the good of all. The *Rules of Civility* were so gentlemanly that they even included regulations concerning suitable table manners and proper conversation.

That Washington appropriated the *Rules of Civility* into his personality and social/political behavior is evident throughout his remaining life. They are cardinal principles of Washington's leadership. An excerpted version of the *Rules of Civility* in somewhat modernized English usage follows.

Rules of Civility

"Let all actions performed in public show some sign of respectful sentiment to the entire company."

When in the presence of others, refrain from touching any part of the body that is not usually within view. The hands and feet are ordinarily visible. In order to form the habit in this point of etiquette, practice it when you are with intimate friends.

Show nothing to your companion that may grieve him, since that might provoke a misunderstanding.

Do not seek amusement by singing to yourself, unless you are beyond the hearing of others; do not tap out the beat of a drum with your hands or feet.

Whenever you cough or sneeze, if you can control these natural efforts, do not sound off so highly or loudly. Do not heave sighs so noisily that others hear. When you yawn, refrain from any sound. Try to avoid yawning altogether when you are in company or engaged in conversation for it is a clear sign of certain weariness with those about you. If you cannot stop from yawning, avoid gaping widely and refrain from speaking while doing. Also, press at your mouth adroitly or turn a little away from the company.

It is an affront and an impertinence to doze while everyone is engaged in conversation, to be seated while the rest stand, or to walk on while others pause, or to speak when you should be silent or listen.

It is not becoming to leave your room while your bed is in disorder, or to dress or undress in the presence of others, or to leave your bedroom half-dressed, half-groomed, or to remain standing in your chamber or at your desk in immodest attire. And although you may have servants to make your bed; nevertheless, take care when you go out of your chamber not to leave your bed uncovered.

It is bad manners in sports, recreation, and at the fireside, to make a new-comer wait very long for a place. Guard against becoming overheated in temperament; don't let excitements carry you away. (Equates excitement with loud speech.)

Do not spit in the fire, nor stoop low before it. Neither put your hands into the flames to warm them, nor set your feet on the fire, especially if there be meat before it. In polite society, do not turn your back to the fire and do not approach it closer than others—for these are the privileges of persons of rank. When there is a need for stirring the fire, putting wood on or pulling or lifting it, this is the job of the person who has the general superintendence of those things.

When seated, place your feet firmly on the ground, with the legs at an equal distance, and neither a leg nor a foot should be crossed one upon the other.

When in public, it is insufferable breach of etiquette to stretch out one's body by extending the arms, or to assume different postures. It is absolutely forbidden to pare your nails in public; and also, do not gnaw your nails.

Do not shake the head, nor fidget the legs, nor roll the eyes, nor frown, nor twist the mouth. Take care not to let saliva escape with your words, and do not let spittle fly into the faces of those with whom you converse. To prevent such an accident, do not approach your conversant too near; but engage in conversation at a reasonable distance.

Do not stop to kill lice or any other disgusting animals of this kind in the presence of your company. If anything on the ground, such as phlegm or spittle, offends the sight, then put your foot on it. If it is on the garment of someone with whom you are conversing, do not show it to him or to anyone else, but do your best to remove it unobserved. If someone obliges you in this way, make your acknowledgments to him.

Turn not your back to others, especially in speaking. Jog not the table or desk on which another reads or writes. Do not lean against anyone, or pull at anyone's clothes while you entertain them in conversation.

Do not stop in conversation to adjust garters or pull up stockings to appear more gallant. Do not allow your nails to be dirty or too long. Take great care for the cleanliness of your hands, but do not overdo it.

It is a very low act to puff up the cheeks, to stick out the tongue, to pull on one's beard, to rub one's hands, to chew or bite on the lips, or to hold the mouth too widely open or too tightly closed.

Do not flatter or wheedle anyone with fine words, for he who aspires to gain another's favor by his honied words shows that the speaker does not regard him in high esteem, and that the speaker deems him far from sensible or clever, in taking him for a man who may be tricked in this manner. Do not play practical jokes on those who would take as an offense.

It is an act directly opposed to good manners to read a book, letters or similar things during ordinary conversation if it is not a pressing matter, or resolved very quickly; and even in that case, it is proper to ask permission unless you are, possibly, the highest in rank of the company. It is even worse to handle other people's work, their books or things of that nature, to get too near to these objects, to look at them closely without the owner's permission, and also to praise or find fault with them before your opinion has been asked; or to approach too close and inconvenience anyone when he is reading his letters or other papers.

The face should not look fantastic, changeable, absent, rapt in attention, covered with sadness, various or volatile; and it should not show any signs of an unquiet mind. On the contrary, it should be open and tranquil, but not too expansive with joy in serious affairs, nor too self-contained by an affected gravity in the ordinary and familiar conversation of human life.

The gestures of the body must be suited to the discourse you are upon.

Reproach none for their infirmities. Avoid it equally when they are natural ones, and do not take pleasure in uttering words that cause anyone shame, whoever it may be.

Show not yourself glad at the misfortune of an another, though he were your enemy. It argues a mischievous mind, that you had a desire to have done it yourself, and if you had the power or opportunity to, you would have.

When you see a crime punished, you may be inwardly pleased; but always show pity to the suffering offender.

Do not laugh too loud or too much at any public spectacle lest you cause yourself to be laughed at.

Superfluous compliments and all affectation of ceremony are to be avoided; yet where due, they are not to be neglected.

In pulling off your hat to persons of distinction, make a reverence, bowing more or less according to the custom of the better bred and quality of persons. Amongst equals, expect not always that they should begin with you first; but to pull off the hat when there is no need is affectation. In the manner of salutation, keep to the most usual custom.

It is ill manners to bid one more eminent than yourself to put on his hat, as well as not to do so when it is due. Likewise, he that makes too much haste to put on his hat does not well, yet he ought to put it on at the first, or at most the second time of being asked. All of these remarks on polite conduct must also be extended to the order to be observed in taking places and in sitting down. Ceremonies without bounds are troublesome.

If anyone comes to speak to you while you are sitting, stand up although he be your inferior. And when you present seats, let it be to everyone according to his rank.

When you meet with one of greater quality than yourself, stop and retire, especially if it be at a door or any straight place, to give way for him to pass.

In walking, the highest place in most countries seems to be on the right hand. Therefore, place yourself on the left of him whom you desire to honor. If three walk together, the middle place is the most honorable. The wall is usually given to the most worthy if two walk together.

If anyone far surpasses others, either in age, estate, or merit, yet in any particular instance would give place to one less than himself (in his own house or elsewhere) the lesser one ought not to accept it. Also, the superior, for fear of making himself uncivil, ought not to press it above once or twice.

To one who is your equal, or not much inferior, you give the chief place in your lodging. And he to whom it is offered ought, at the first to refuse, but at the second offer to accept, though not without acknowledging his own unworthiness.

They that are in dignity or in office have, in all places, precedency. But while they are young, they ought to respect those that are their equals in birth or other qualities, even though they have no public charge.

It is the height of politeness always to speak better of those with whom we converse than of ourselves. Particularly when they are persons of a superior rank to ourselves, with whom we ought never to dispute in any fashion.

Let your discourse with men of business be short and comprehensive. One should spare them and make himself understood rather by looks than by words.

Craftsman and persons of low degree ought not to use many ceremonies to disturb their superiors or others of high rank, but respect and honor them. Those of high rank ought to treat their lessers with affability and courtesy, without arrogancy.

In speaking to men of quality, do not lean, nor look them full in the face, nor approach too near them. At the least, keep a full step in distance.

In visiting the sick, do not act the physician if you are not trained in that science.

In writing or speaking, give to every person his due title, according to his degree and the custom of the place.

Strive not with your superiors in argument, but always submit your judgment to others with modesty.

Undertake not to teach your equal in the art that he himself professes. It flavours of arrogancy.

Let your ceremonies in courtesy be proper to the dignity of the place of the person with whom you converse. It is absurd to act the same with a clown and a Prince.

Do not express joy before one who is sick or in pain, for that contrary passion will aggravate his misery.

When a man does all he can, though it succeeds not well, blame not he that did it since he is more worthy of praise than blame.

To advise or reprehend anyone, consider whether it ought to be public or in private, presently or at some other time, in what terms to do it and, in reproving, show no signs of choler, but do it with all sweetness and mildness.

Take all admonitions thankfully, in what time or place whatsoever given, but afterwards, not being culpable, take a time or place convenient to let him know it that gave them.

Mock not, nor jest at anything of importance. Make no jests that are sharp and biting, and if you deliver anything witty and pleasant, abstain from laughing thereat yourself.

Wherein you reprove another, be unblameful yourself. Example is more prevalent than precept.

Use no reproachful language against anyone. Neither curse nor revile.

Do not be hasty to believe flying reports to the disparagement of any one.

Wear not your clothes foul, ripped or dusty, but see to it that they be brushed once every day at least. Take heed that you approach not to any uncleanness.

In your apparel, be modest and endeavor to accommodate nature rather than procure admiration. Keep to the fashion of your equals, such as are civil and orderly, with respect to times and places.

Run not in the streets. Neither go too slowly nor with mouth open. Go not shaking your arms, stamping or shuffling, nor pull up your stockings in the street. Walk not upon your toes, nor in a dancing or skipping manner, nor yet with measured steps. Strike not the heels together, nor stoop when there is no occasion.

Play not the peacock, looking everywhere about you to see if you be well decked, if your shoes fit well, if your stockings sit neatly, and your clothes appear handsomely.

Eat not in the streets, nor in your house out of the normal meal times; at least abstain from it in the presence of others.

Associate yourself with men of good quality if you esteem your own reputation. For 'tis better to be alone than in bad company.

In walking about the house alone with a person whose rank demands some deference, at the first step be sure to give him your right hand. Stop not walking until he does. Do not be the first to turn. If you do turn, let it be with your face towards him. If he be a man of great quality, walk not with him cheek by jowl but somewhat behind him, but yet in such a manner that he may easily speak to you.

Let your conversation be without malice or envy, for 'tis a sign of a tractable and commendable nature. And in all causes of passion admit reason to govern.

Never express anything unbecoming, nor act against moral Rules, especially in front of your inferiors.

Be not immodest in urging your friends to discover their secrets.

Utter not base or frivolous things amongst grave and learned men; nor very difficult questions or subjects, nor things hard to be believed, among the ignorant. Stuff not your discourse with proverbs when you are amongst your betters or your equals.

Speak not of sad things in a time of mirth, or at the table. Speak not of melancholy things such as death and wounds, and if others mention them, change the discourse if you can. Tell not your dreams but to your intimate friends.

A man ought not to value himself of his achievements or rare qualities, his riches, his titles, his virtue or his kindred. But he need not speak meanly of himself either.

Jesting must be avoided when it is inappropriate. Laugh not aloud, nor at all without occasion. Deride no man's misfortune, although there may seem to be some cause.

Speak not injurious words, neither in jest nor earnest. Scoff at no one, although they give occasion.

Be not rude, but friendly and courteous. Be the first to salute, to hear, to answer; and be not pensive when it is time to converse.

Detract not from others; neither be excessive in commending them.

Go not thither where you know not whether you shall be welcome or not. Give not advice without being asked and, when desired, do it briefly.

If two contend together, take not the part of either unless some greater reason obliges you to do so. And be not obstinate in your opinion. In things to which you are indifferent, be a part of the majority.

Reprehend not the imperfections of others for that is the province of parents, masters, superiors.

Gaze not at the marks or blemishes of others, and ask not how they came. What you may speak in secret to your friend, deliver not before others.

Speak not in an unknown tongue in company, but in your own language as those of quality do, and not as the vulgar world would. Sublime matters treat seriously.

Think before you speak. Pronounce not imperfectly nor bring out your words too hastily, but orderly and distinctly.

When another speaks, be attentive yourself and disturb not the audience. If any hesitate in his words, help him not, nor prompt him without it being desired; interrupt him not, nor answer him until his speech be ended.

In the midst of discourse, ask not what it is about. But if you perceive any stop because of your arrival, rather, request the speaker to continue. If a person of quality comes in while you converse, it is gracious to repeat what was said before.

While you are talking, point not with your finger at him whom you discourse, nor approach too near to whom you talk, especially to his face.

Treat with men at fit times about business, and whisper not in the company of others.

Make no comparisons, and if any of the company be commended for any brave act or virtue, commend not another for the same.

Be not apt to relate news if you know not the truth thereof. In discoursing of things that you have heard, name not your author. Do not reveal a secret.

Be not tedious in discourse or in reading, unless you find the company to be pleased therewith.

Be not curious to know the affairs of others. Do not approach near to those who speak in private.

Undertake not what you cannot perform. Be careful to keep your promises.

When you fulfill a mission, do it without passion and with discretion, however mean the person be for whom you do it.

When your superiors talk, listen eagerly and neither speak nor laugh.

In the company of those of higher quality than yourself, speak not until you are asked a question. Then stand upright, put off your hat, and answer in a few words.

In disputes, be not so desirous to overcome objections as not to give liberty to each one to deliver his opinion, and submit to the judgment of the majority, especially if they are judges of the dispute.

Let your bearing be such as becomes a man who is grave, settled and attentive to what is said, without being too serious. Contradict not at every turn what others say.

Be not tedious in discourse; make not many digressions; nor repeat often the same manner of discourse.

Speak not evil of those who are absent, for it is unjust.

When dining, scratch not, neither spit, cough nor blow your nose, except when there is a necessity for it.

Make no show of taking great delight in your food. Feed not with greediness. Cut your bread with a knife. Lean not on the table. Do not find fault with what you have to eat.

Take no salt, nor cut bread when your knife is greasy.

When entertaining someone, it is polite to serve him at table and present the dishes of food to him. When invited by another, it is more polite to wait to be served by the host, or someone else unless invited by the host to help himself to the food. Avoid being officious in helping others when not in one's own house, where one has little authority unless the host cannot attend to everything. In that case, help the ones nearest.

If you soak bread in the sauce, let it be no more than what you put in your mouth at one time. Blow not on your broth at the table, but wait until it cools of itself.

Put not your meat to your mouth with your knife in your hand. Neither spit forth the stones of any fruit pie upon a dish, nor cast anything under the table.

It is not polite to stoop too close into one's meat. Keep fingers clean, and when foul, wipe them on a corner of your table napkin.

Put not another bite into your mouth until the former be swallowed. Let not your morsels be too big for your jowls.

Drink not, nor talk with your mouth full. Neither gaze about while you are drinking.

Drink not too leisurely, nor yet too hastily. Wipe your lips before and after drinking. Breath not when drinking, or ever with too great a noise for it is uncivil.

Cleanse not your teeth with the tablecloth, napkin, fork or knife; but if others do it, let it be done with a tooth pick.

Rinse not your mouth in the presence of others.

It is out of fashion to call upon others often to eat. Nor need you drink to others every time you eat.

In the company of your betters, be not longer in eating than they are. Lay not your arm, but arise with only a touch on the end of the table.

The most distinguished member of the company is first to unfold his napkin and touch the food. The rest should graciously wait without touching the food before he does.

Be not angry at table, whatsoever happens, and if you have reason to be so, show it not. Put on a cheerful countenance, especially if there be strangers, for good humor makes one dish of meat a feast.

Do not place yourself at the head of the table unless it be your due or the master of the house would have it so. Contend not lest you should trouble the company.

If others talk at table, be attentive. But talk not with meat in your mouth.

When you speak of God or His attributes, be serious and speak with words of reverence. Honor and obey your natural parents, although they may be poor.

Let your recreations be manful, and not sinful.

Labor to keep alive in your breast that little spark of celestial fire called conscience."

George Washington was a wise friend to more diverse Americans than any other man of his times. A modern biographer observes:

"He knew officers, generals and privates; Frenchmen and Englishmen; Yankees and Southern planters; frontiersmen and Quakers. He dealt with Indians who were enemies and Indians who were allies; with blacks who were slaves, who were freemen, and who were his own soldiers. His ability to deal with all of them was founded on his training in these rules [110 Rules for Young Gentlemen, also known as The Rules of Civility]."[22]

America's civility is rooted deep in spirituality.

CHAPTER TWO

Washington's Prayers

*"That an All Powerful Providence may keep us both
in safety is the prayer of your ever faithful and
affectionate Friend."*[23]
—George Washington

small manuscript book entitled "Daily Sacrifice,"
all in the handwriting of twenty year old George
Washington, was sold at auction by Washington's heirs
in Philadelphia on April 21, 1891. The most hallowed
of all his writings, these remnants of Washington's personal prayer book are written on twenty-four pages of a
small journal about the size of an ordinary pocket mem-
orandum. No one knows whether these prayers were
originals or if Washington copied them from another
source.[24] It is common knowledge that Washington
prayed these prayers twice daily each day of the week.

Washington's daily prayers enriched his faith as he sought holiness and happiness. Such faith is a gift from God and like all living things, it must be nurtured if it is to grow. Washington, realizing he was expected to remain faithful to God's Plan for him throughout all of life's stages and challenges, called to God always, bent to God's ways as revealed in Scripture, blessed God in good times and in adversity.

Washington believed that God's mercy is His reward for those who seek Him. He recognized every man as a redeemed child of God's love whether he knew Jesus by name or not. Washington was aware that no one knows Jesus unless the Eternal Father reveals His Son. Washington, though he feared God, trusted that God is our Father Most Loving. Steeped in that wisdom, Washington dared not interfere in God's timetable of revelation. He profoundly respected every man's authentic faith revelation, though God's Son, Jesus Christ, was the Light of Washington's life.

Washington cherished his Christian heritage enough to live it to the fullest. Though he clung to no contemporary, Washington clung steadfastly to Jesus Christ. Washington's life experiences convinced him that human nature is good, but flawed. Consequently, he prayed much, seeking continuous grace to help his human acts achieve goodness and justice and triumph over every sort of defeat.

Washington's prayers unveil his own humble and contrite heart which God did not spurn. Washington's prayers drew down God's mercy for the American people in the past. Today, they ennoble people who sincerely pray them.

George Washington's Sunday Morning Prayer

Almighty God, and most merciful Father,
who didst command the children of Israel to offer a daily sacrifice to Thee,
that thereby they might glorify and praise Thee for Thy protection both night and day;
receive, O Lord, my morning sacrifice which I now offer up to Thee;
I yield Thee humble and hearty thank that Thou hast preserved me from the dangers of the night past,
and brought me to the light of this day,
and the comforts thereof,
a day which is consecrated to Thine own service and for Thine own honor.
Let my heart therefore, Gracious God,
be so affected with the glory and majesty of it,

that I may not do mine own works, but wait on Thee, and discharge those weighty duties Thou requirest of me;

and since Thou art a God of pure eyes,

and wilt be sanctified in all who draw near unto Thee, who doest not regard the sacrifice of fools,

nor hear sinners who tread in Thy courts,

pardon, I beseech Thee, my sins,

remove them from Thy presence,

as far as the east is from the west,

and accept of me for the merits of Thy son Jesus Christ,

that when I come into Thy temple,

and compass Thy altar,

my prayers may come before Thee as incense;

and as Thou wouldst hear me calling upon Thee in my prayers, so give me grace to hear Thee calling on me in Thy Word, that it may bring wisdom, righteousness, reconciliation and peace to the saving of my soul in the day of the Lord Jesus.

Grant that I may hear it with reverence,

receive it with meekness, mingle it with faith,

and that it may accomplish in me, Gracious God, the good work for which Thou hast sent it.

Bless my family, kindred, friends, and country,

be our God & guide this day and forever for His sake, who lay down in the Grave and arose again for us,

Jesus Christ our Lord. Amen.

George Washington's Sunday Evening Prayer

O most glorious God, in Jesus Christ my merciful and loving father,

I acknowledge and confess my guilt, in the weak and imperfect performance of the duties of this day.

I have called on Thee for pardon and forgiveness of sins, but so coldly and carelessly, that my prayers are become my sin

and stand in need of pardon.

I have heard Thy Holy Word, but with such deadness of spirit that I have been an unprofitable and forgetful hearer, so that O Lord, tho' I have done Thy work

yet it hath been so negligently

that I may rather expect a curse than a blessing from Thee.

But, O God, who art rich in mercy and plenteous in redemption,

mark not, I beseech Thee, what I have done amiss; remember that I am but dust, and remit my transgressions, negligence & ignorance, and cover them all with the absolute obedience of Thy dear Son,

that those sacrifices which I have offered

may be accepted by Thee, in and for the sacrifice of Jesus Christ offered upon the cross for me;

for His sake, ease me of the burdens of my sins,

and give me grace that by the call of the Gospel

I may rise from the slumber of sin into the newness of life.

Let me live according to those holy rules which

Thou hast this day prescribed in Thy Holy Word.

Make me to know what is acceptable in Thy sight, and therein to delight.

Open the eyes of my understanding,

and help me thoroughly to examine myself

concerning my knowledge, faith and repentance.

Increase my faith, and direct me to the true object, Jesus Christ, the way, the truth and the life.

Bless O Lord all the people of this land,

from the highest to the lowest, particularly those whom Thou hast appointed to rule over us in church and state.

Continue Thy goodness to me this night.

"*Washington, always beloved as a citizen, an officer and a gentleman, is America's mystical icon of heroic grace.*"

2   "...Martha Washington was the ideal woman for the new American republic. She was no[t]
born of the aristocracy, but she gained the admiration and respect of all classes of people."

3   "In 1745, sixteen-year-old George came to live at Mount Vernon. This serendipity
gave young George a life of culture and connections."

These weak petitions I humbly implore Thee to hear, accept and answer for the sake of Thy dear Son Jesus Christ, our Lord. Amen.

* * *

George Washington's Monday Morning Prayer

O Eternal and everlasting God,

I presume to present myself this morning before Thy Divine majesty

and beseech Thee to accept of my humble and hearty thanks, that it has pleased Thy great goodness to keep and preserve me this night from all the dangers poor mortals are subject to.

Thou has given me sweet and pleasant sleep, whereby I find my body refreshed and comforted for performing the duties of this day,

in which I beseech Thee to defend me from all perils of body and soul.

Direct my thoughts, words and work.

Wash away my sins in the immaculate blood of the Lamb.

Purge my heart by Thy Holy Spirit, from the dross of my natural corruption, that I may with more freedom of mind and liberty of will serve Thee, the ever lasting God,

in righteous and holiness this day, and all the days of my life.

Increase my faith in the sweet promises of the Gospel;

give me repentance from dead works;

pardon my wanderings and direct my thoughts unto Thyself, the God of my salvation.

Teach me how to live in Thy fear, labor in Thy service, and ever to run in the ways on Thy commandments.

Make me always watchful over my heart,

that neither the terrors of conscience, the loathing of holy duties, the love of sin, nor an unwillingness to depart this life, may cast me into a spiritual slumber.

But daily frame me more and more into the likeness of Thy Son, Jesus Christ,

that living in Thy fear, and dying in Thy favor,

I may in Thy appointed time attain the Resurrection of the just unto eternal life.

Bless my family, friends and kindred.

Unite us all in praising and glorifying Thee in all our works begun, continued, and ended when we shall come to make our last account before Thee, Blessed Savior, who has taught us thus to pray.

Our Father, who art in Heaven, hallowed be Thy Name.

Thy Kingdom come.

Thy will be done on earth as it is in Heaven.

Give us this day our daily bread.

Forgive us our trespasses as we forgive those who trespass against us.

Lead us not into temptation but deliver us from evil.

For Thine is the Kingdom, the power and the glory forever. Amen.

* * *

George Washington's Monday Evening Prayer

Most gracious Lord God, from whom proceedeth every good and perfect gift,

I offer to Thy Divine Majesty my unfeigned praise and thanksgiving for all Thy mercies toward me.

Thou made me at first and hast ever since sustained the work of Thine own hand.

Thou gave Thy Son to die for me,

and hast given me assurance of salvation upon my repentance and sincerely endeavoring to conform my life to His holy precepts and example.

Thou art pleased to lengthen out to me the time of repentance

and to move me to it by Thy Spirit and by Thy Word,

by Thy mercies and by Thy judgments.

Out of a deepness of Thy mercies, and my own unworthiness

I do appear before Thee at this time.

I have sinned and done very wickedly,

be merciful to me O, God, and pardon me for Jesus Christ sake.

Instruct me in the particulars on my duty.

Suffer me not to be tempted above what Thou has given me strength to bear.

Take care, I pray Thee, of my affairs and more and more direct me in Thy truth.

Defend me from my enemies, especially my spiritual ones. Suffer me not to be drawn from Thee, by the blandishments of the world, carnal desires, the cunning of the devil, or deceitfulness of sin.

Work in me Thy good will and pleasure,

and discharge my mind from all things that are displeasing to Thee,

of all ill will and discontent, wrath and bitterness, pride and vain conceit of myself and render me charitable, pure, holy, patient and heavenly minded.

Be with me at the hour of death; dispose me for it, and deliver me from the slavish fear of it.

Make me willing and fit to die whenever Thou shall call me hence.

Bless our rulers in Church and State.

Bless O Lord the whole race of mankind, and let the world be filled with the knowledge of Thee and Thy Son, Jesus Christ.

Pity the sick, the poor, the weak, the needy, the widows and fatherless, and all that mourn or are broken in heart, and be merciful to them according to their several necessities.

Bless my friends and give me grace to forgive my enemies as heartily as I desire forgiveness of Thee my Heavenly Father.

I beseech Thee to defend me this night from all evil, and do more for me than I can think to ask, for Jesus Christ's sake, in whose most holy name and words, I continue to pray.

Our Father, who art in Heaven, hallowed be Thy Name.

Thy Kingdom come.

Thy will be done on earth as it is in Heaven.

Give us this day our daily bread.

Forgive us our trespasses as we forgive those who trespass against us.

Lead us not into temptation but deliver us from evil.

For Thine is the Kingdom, the power and the glory forever. Amen.

* * *

George Washington's Tuesday Morning Prayer

O Lord our God, most mighty and merciful Father,

I Thine unworthy creature and servant, do once more approach Thy presence.

Though not worthy to appear before Thee because of my natural corruptions,

and the many sins and transgressions which I have committed against Thy divine majesty,

yet I beseech Thee, for the sake of Him in whom Thou are well pleased, the Lord Jesus Christ,

to admit me to render Thee deserved thanks and praises for Thy manifold mercies extended toward me,

for the quiet rest and repose of the past night,

for food, raiment, health, peace, liberty, and the hopes of a better life through the merits of Thy dear Son's bitter passion.

O kind Father, continue Thy mercy and favor to me this day and ever hereafter.

Prosper all my lawful undertakings.

Let me have all my directions from Thy Holy Spirit, and success from Thy bountiful hand.

Let the bright beams of Thy light so shine into my heart, and enlighten my mind in understanding Thy blessed word, that I may be enabled to perform Thy will in all things,

and effectually resist all temptations of the world, the flesh and the devil.

Preserve and defend our rulers in Church and State.

Bless the people of this land.

Be a father to the fatherless,

a comforter to the comfortless,

a deliverer to the captives and a physician to the sick.

Let Thy blessings be upon our friends, kindred and families. Be our guide this day and forever through Jesus Christ,

in whose blessed form of prayer I conclude my weak petitions.

Our Father, who art in Heaven, hallowed be Thy Name.

Thy Kingdom come.

Thy will be done on earth as it is in Heaven.

Give us this day our daily bread.

Forgive us our trespasses as we forgive those who trespass against us.

Lead us not into temptation but deliver us from evil.

For Thine is the Kingdom, the power and the glory forever. Amen.

* * *

George Washington's Tuesday Evening Prayer

Most gracious God and Heavenly Father,

we cannot cease, but must cry unto Thee for mercy, because my sins cry against me for justice.

How shall I address myself unto Thee.

I must with the publican stand and admire at Thy great goodness, tender mercy, and long suffering toward me,

in that Thou has kept me the past day from being consumed and brought to naught.

O Lord, what is man, or the son of man, that Thou regardest him.

The more days pass over my head the more sins and iniquities I heap up against Thee.

If I should cast up the account of my good deeds done this day, how few and small they would be.

But if I should reckon my transgressions, surely they would be many and great.

O blessed Father,

let Thy Son's blood wash me from all impurities,

and cleanse me from the stains of sin that are upon me.

Give me grace to lay hold upon His merits,

that they may be my reconciliation and atonement unto Thee—that I may know my sins are forgiven by His passion and death.

Embrace me in the arms of Thy mercy.

Vouchsafe to receive me unto the bosom of Thy love.

Shadow me with Thy wings,

that I may safely rest under Thy protection this night.

And so unto Thy hands I commend myself, both soul and body, in the name of Thy Son, Jesus Christ,

beseeching Thee, when this life shall end,

I may take my everlasting rest with Thee in Thy heavenly Kingdom.

Bless all in authority over us.

Be merciful with all those afflicted with Thy cross or calamity.

Bless all my friends, forgive all my enemies

and accept my thanksgiving this evening for the mercies and favors afforded me.

Hear and graciously answer these my requests,

and whatever else Thou see needful grant us,

for the sake of Jesus Christ in whose blessed name and words I continue to pray.

Our Father, who art in Heaven, hallowed be Thy Name.

Thy Kingdom come.

Thy will be done on earth as it is in Heaven.

Give us this day our daily bread.

Forgive us our trespasses as we forgive those who trespass against us.

Lead us not into temptation but deliver us from evil.

For Thine is the Kingdom, the power and the glory forever. Amen.

* * *

George Washington's Wednesday Morning Prayer

Almighty and eternal Lord God,
the great Creator of Heaven and earth,

and the God and Father of our Lord Jesus Christ,

look down from Heaven, in pity and compassion upon me Thy servant,

who humbly prostrate myself before Thee,

sensible of Thy mercy and my own misery.

There is an infinite distance between Thy glorious majesty and me, Thy poor creature, the work of Thy hand,

between Thy infinite power, and my weakness,

Thy wisdom and my folly,

Thy eternal Being, and my mortal frame.

But O Lord, I have set myself at a greater distance from Thee by my sin and wickedness,

and humbly acknowledge the corruption of my nature and the many rebellions of my life.

I have sinned against heaven and before Thee,

in thought, word and deed.

I have contemned Thy majesty and holy laws.

I have likewise sinned by omitting what I ought to have done, and committing what I ought not.

I have rebelled against light, despised Thy mercies and judgments, and broken my vows and promises.

I have neglected the means of Grace and opportunities of becoming better.

My iniquities are multiplied and my sins are very great.

I confess them, O Lord, with shame and sorrow, detestation and loathing,

and desire to be vile in my own eyes, as I have rendered myself vile in Thine.

I humbly beseech Thee to be merciful to me in the free pardon of my sins,

for the sake of Thy dear Son, my only Savior, Jesus Christ, who came not to call the righteous, but sinners to repentance.

Be pleased to renew my nature and write Thy laws upon my heart.

Help me to live righteously, soberly, and godly in this evil world.

Make me humble, meek, patient, and contented,

and work in me the grace of Thy Holy Spirit.

Prepare me for death and judgment,

and let the thoughts thereof awaken me to greater care and study to approve myself unto Thee in well doing.

Bless our rulers in church and State.

Help all in affliction or adversity—give them patience and a sanctified use of their affliction,

and in Thy good time, deliverance from them.

Forgive my enemies, take me unto Thy protection this day. Keep me in perfect peace, which I ask in the name and for the sake of Jesus in whose name I pray.

Our Father, who art in Heaven, hallowed be Thy Name.

Thy Kingdom come.

Thy will be done on earth as it is in Heaven.

Give us this day our daily bread.

Forgive us our trespasses as we forgive those who trespass against us.

Lead us not into temptation but deliver us from evil.

For Thine is the Kingdom, the power and the glory forever.

Amen.

* * *

George Washington's Wednesday Evening Prayer

Holy and eternal Lord God who art the King of Heaven,

and the watchman of Israel,

that never slumberest or sleepest,

what shall we render unto Thee for all Thy benefits.

Because Thou hast inclined Thine ears unto me,

therefore will I call on Thee as long as I live.

From the rising of the sun to the going down of the same, let Thy name be praised.

Among the infinite riches of Thy mercy towards me,

I desire to render thanks and praise for Thy merciful preservation of me this day,

as well as all the days of my life,

and for Thy many other blessings and mercies, spiritual and temporal which Thou hast bestowed upon me,

contrary to my deserving.

All these Thy mercies call on me to be thankful

and my infirmities and wants call for a continuance of Thy tender mercies.

Cleanse my soul O Lord, I beseech Thee,

from whatever is offensive to Thee, and hurtful to me,

and give me what is convenient for me.

Watch over me this night,

and give me comfortable and sweet sleep to fit me for the service of the day following.

Let my soul watch for the coming of the Lord Jesus.

Let my bed put me in mind of my grave,

and my rising from there of my last Resurrection.

O Heavenly Father, so frame this heart of mine,

that I may ever delight to live according to Thy will and command,

in holiness and righteousness before Thee all the days of my life.

Let me remember O Lord,

the time will come when the trumpet shall sound,

and the dead shall arise and stand before the judgment seat, and give an account of whatever they have
done in the body. Let me so prepare my soul that I may
do it with joy

and not with grief

Bless the rulers and people of this land

and forget not those who are under any affliction
or oppression.

Let Thy favor be extended to all my relations,
friends, and all others who I ought to remember in
my prayers.

Hear me I beseech Thee

for the sake of my dear Redeemer in whose holy
words, I farther pray.

Our Father, who art in Heaven, hallowed be
Thy Name.

Thy Kingdom come.

Thy will be done on earth as it is in Heaven.

Give us this day our daily bread.

Forgive us our trespasses as we forgive those who
trespass against us.

Lead us not into temptation but deliver us from evil.

For Thine is the Kingdom, the power and the glory
forever. Amen.

* * *

George Washington's Thursday Morning Prayer

Most gracious Lord God, whose dwelling is in the highest heavens,

and yet beholdest the lowly and humble upon earth,

I blush and am ashamed to lift up my eyes to Thy dwelling place,

because I have sinned against Thee.

Look down I beseech Thee upon me, Thine unworthy servant

who prostrate myself at the footstool of Thy mercy, confessing my own guiltiness,

and begging pardon for my sins.

What couldst Thou have done Lord more for me,

or what could I have done more against Thee?

Thou didst send me Thy Son to take our nature upon-

* * *

The manuscript ended here at the close of that page. Unfortunately, other pages have not yet been found. It is hoped that if they still exist, they will be brought forth in these times for the glory of God and the edification of people throughout the world.

CHAPTER THREE

Washington's Early Military Experience

"Good moral character is the first essential in a man."[25]
—George Washington

*G*eorge Washington looked to his elder half-brother Lawrence for guidance and economic assistance during his adolescence. A few months after his father Augustine's death, in 1743, Lawrence married Anne Fairfax, the daughter of Virginia land magnate Colonel William Fairfax, proprietor of millions of acres of colonial property. He brought his bride to live at the estate he inherited from his father at Little Hunting Creek on the Potomac River. Lawrence named his home Mount

Vernon, in honor of his Commanding Officer, Admiral Edward Vernon, under whom he had served as an officer in 1741, during the British siege of the Spanish Caribbean port of Cartagena.

In 1745, sixteen-year-old George came to live at Mount Vernon. This serendipity gave young George a life of culture and connections. "George was welcomed not only at Mount Vernon but at Belvoir [the Fairfax estate], as well. Indeed, Belvoir became something of a finishing school for George in his impressionable teenage years, and he learned first hand how the elite of Virginia society conducted themselves. With its handsome and commodious rooms adorned by luxurious carpets and rich furniture imported from England, Belvoir was one of the finest homes in the colony."[26]

At age sixteen George was:

"...physically his father's son and, in strength, almost a man. He was systematic, he had achieved his ambition of learning to write swiftly and clearly, and he could perform readily enough the simple mathematical problems of surveying. His mind found interest chiefly in matters of business, concerning which he was mature beyond his age, though he had little imagination except for planning how he could advance himself...He rode admirably. He made on adults an excellent impression of vitality, courtesy and integrity at the same time that he won the good will of the young. Along with these excellencies, he had the softness of the young gentleman who would ride horseback by the hour but always would come back to a comfortable house and a good bed. Although he was far from rich, he was accustomed to an ease quite different from the life of the frontier. Instead of wearing a hunting shirt and telling time 'by sun' he carried a watch and enjoyed some of the clothes of fashion."[27]

George Washington's life of ease would be short-lived, though his refined taste would help build a new nation out of the harsh wilderness.

His first job at seventeen was as the youngest surveyor ever appointed in Virginia; he became the official surveyor for the County of Culpepper. In this position George learned how to survive on the frontier. He also became adept at recognizing the value of fine real estate. By the time he was twenty years old, and earning about 100 pounds a year, George purchased 2,000 acres of land in the Shenandoah Valley.

Upon Lawrence's untimely death from tuberculosis in 1752, twenty-two year old George was appointed to his half-brother's position as military adjutant for the Southern District of Virginia, and subsequently for the Northern Neck and Eastern Shore.[28] George rented Mount Vernon from his deceased brother's widow. Lawrence had provided in his will that his property at Mount Vernon would pass to his wife and then to their living children. If none would survive, Lawrence devised to his young brother George a reversionary interest in Mount Vernon.[29] Consequently, after the death of his sister-in-law, all of whose four children had predeceased her, George Washington acquired title to Mount Vernon.

Because of his limited financial means, George did not attend college, though his father and three elder half brothers had been educated in England.[30] Washington's mother may not have approved of the value of higher education because of her own limited means, and she may have expected her first born son to be a provider.

Driven, motivated, and self-taught, Washington developed his character through his love of manly sports and long hours in the vast wilderness on horse-back as a surveyor and military leader. No stranger to letters, Washington enjoyed the erudition of Stoic philosophy, especially Plutarch's *Lives*, Addison's *Cato* and Seneca's *Dialogues*.[31] These works, coupled with his prayer life rooted in the Bible filled his mind and soul with dreams and goals.

Washington's bold horsemanship, modesty and excellence at hunting fox endeared him to the Fairfax family. He continued to pass many happy hours at Belvoir enjoying the expertise and business acumen of Lord Fairfax. George suspected that great profits await-ed settlers beyond the Allegheny Mountains and Lord Fairfax encouraged Washington to seek his fortune in the western wilderness.

During his early western travels, Washington found vast tracts of rich, fertile land, magnificent fruit-filled trees, and rivers and streams sparkling with fish. He observed Indian customs, and their weakness for hard liquor. As a young Major in the Virginia Militia, Washington had many encounters with wary tribal chiefs. He appreciated and respected the native tribes' attachment to these bountiful lands and waters.

Washington's family along with other prominent Virginia families owned shares in the Ohio Company of

Virginia which held a grant in the Ohio River Basin. The French government, desiring to shore up its position from the Ohio Valley into French Canada, sent troops to occupy the territory. French Canada, whose population at that time numbered less than sixty thousand farmers, fishermen and fur traders, was also attempting to acquire as yet unsettled land along the Ohio River. Consequently, under the command of Marquis Du Quesne, a French Canadian fort stood at the confluence of the Allegheny and Monongahela Rivers, which rivers merge to form the Ohio River.

At age twenty-two, when Washington was commissioned Lieutenant-Colonel of the Virginia Militia, Governor Dinwiddie assigned him to the western frontier. Dinwiddie decided to send English colonial forces into the Ohio Valley with his instructions to the French to depart and he chose Washington to deliver his orders. Accordingly, on November 23, 1753, Lieutenant Colonel George Washington arrived at the French stronghold of Fort Du Quesne.

Commanding one hundred fifty men, Washington encountered a hopeless military situation at the Fort. Though the French proved too intimidating for the Virginia Militia, Washington learned much spiritually and diplomatically during that deployment.

Significantly, he acquired invaluable knowledge of guerrilla warfare as practiced by the Native Americans of that region. This knowledge would later help him to turn the tide of defeat during the Revolutionary War.

The young Virginian instinctively relied on moral force when he encountered difficulties. This endeared him to the Indian leaders of the Ohio Valley whom he met during that deployment. The local Indian "Half King" let it be known that he discerned spiritual greatness in young Washington and gave him the Indian name Caunotaucarius—which means Towntaker.

During the expedition, Washington had a narrow brush with death in the vicinity of the French Fort LeBoeuf, (near Erie, Pennsylvania). As young Washington and an aide took a shortcut through dense woods, they came upon a party of French Indians who ambushed them. One of the prowling Indians fired directly at Washington's chest. Washington said of the incident that he was "not fifteen steps off..."[32] A legend survives that at that close range, the bullets did not harm Washington, who merely brushed gun powder off his uniform while the firing Indian instantly fell on his knees to worship the giant his shotgun would not kill. Young George, a man of humor and quick wit, instinctively reached forward and lifted the quaking warrior to his feet. "I am a man just like you", he reassured the frightened Indian.

Washington wrote further of the incident.

"We took this fellow into custody...Then let him go and walked all the remaining part of the night."[33]

Washington's superior rank allowed him to over rule his aide who insistently demanded that the Indian be killed lest he follow them and complete his lethal work.

Though Washington had delivered Governor Dinwiddie's instructions to the French commandant, the Chevalier de St. Pierre, he met with no success. Washington's reports to Governor Dinwiddie on French plans, arms and Indian alliances however were so impressive that the Governor rushed them into print for attention not only in the colonies, but also in London.

By the spring of 1755, the aristocratic Major General Edward Braddock, Commander in Chief of the King of England's North American Forces commissioned young George Washington a Captain of North American Forces, the highest position he had authority to fill in the colonies. Washington, by now highly familiar with the terrain and dangers imposed by the untamed wilderness beyond Western Maryland,

explained the perils of an expedition to General
Braddock. However, the patrician General summarily
dismissed Washington's knowledge and opinions of the
western front. Nonetheless, on May 10, 1755, General
Braddock appointed Captain George Washington his
aid de camp. As such, he would accompany Braddock
and his forces in their military campaign to capture Fort
Du Quesne and open the Western lands.

The hardship of the march over the Allegheny
Mountains far exceeded the expectations of the English
General. He had underestimated the distance, the
harshness of the land, the cruelty of the weather and
the steep difficulties of the mountains. Wagons simply
could not haul their loads. Mud and rains joined their
fury to stall the British march.

Along the way, Captain Washington providentially
became quite ill. Bloody dysentery, perhaps from pol-
luted water, infected many of the soldiers. Not to be
deterred, Braddock decided to send a single detachment supported by artillery ahead to Fort Du Quesne.
Young Washington desperately longed to be among the
regiment who would plant the flag of England on
French soil at Fort Du Quesne; instead, sick with
dysentery, fever, pain and weakness, he remained con-
fined to his cot. Debilitating illness continued to keep

George prostrate in the back of a wagon until a physician had the presence of mind to administer a patent medicine that gradually alleviated Washington's problem. He then proceeded in the back of a moving wagon toward the front. Messages abounded of Indian massacres, colonial families being scalped and slain. Still too weak to ride horseback, George continued toward the front by covered wagon.

The possibility of participating in the liberation of Fort Du Quesne drove Washington's valiant efforts in crossing the rough terrain to the battle site. The military plan was to get troops, artillery and wagons across the Monongahela River and on to victory at the nearby Fort. George was twenty-three years old, unaccustomed to weakness yet powerless over his physical problem. As he neared the battlefront, he worried that he could not endure the jolts of a warrior horse.

Captain Washington's job required him to be mounted and afield at the charge on Fort Du Quesne. Severe dysentery causes certain rawness. To lessen his pain, Washington procured several pillows and tied them to his saddle. Little did he know then how this fortuity would save his life and help to launch his legend.

The English militia had never before fought a coalition of Indians and French using guerrilla tactics.

General Braddock continued to disregard young Washington's experienced counsel about warfare on the Western frontier. His Royal troops were untrained to fight an enemy they could not see. Suddenly, war whoops from invisible warriors they had never before heard chilled their veins. The British soldiers broke ranks. Into this chaos rode General Braddock accompanied by his aid de camp George Washington perched high on his pillow-laden saddle.

The brutal battle quickly escalated into ferocious combat. George somehow managed to stay in his saddle, despite his weakness. His tall 6' 4" figure was an easy mark for the hidden riflemen. When his horse was shot out from under him, Washington found another, remounted, pillows and all, and made his way to the front. A second time his horse was shot from under him, and he again found another to mount. An unseen rifleman fired at his face and pierced his hat. Two more bullets scorched through his hat. But Washington rode on, seated high on his pillows and focusing on his job. Then, hot lead pierced his uniform, but he remained untouched. Eyewitnesses were both stunned and frightened. The myth of George Washington as an American Achilles was born at that battle.

Washington wrote of that battle experience.

"By the all powerful dispensations of Providence,
I have been protected beyond all human proba-
bility or expectation, for I had four bullets
through my coat, and two horses shot under me,
yet escaped unhurt, although death was leveling
my companions on every side of me." [34]

Suddenly, General Braddock fell to the ground as
bullets crashed through his right arm and penetrated
his lung. The fiendish whoop of the savages frightened
Braddock's soldiers even more and led them to panic.
Washington quickly responded. His job was to take his
fallen Commander in Chief across the river and out of
the line of fire. He commandeered a small wagon to
transport the severely wounded Major General. Under
intense fire, Washington personally conveyed his suffering leader across the ford.

Indians pounced onto the battlefield and competed
with vultures to plunder the dead, scalp the wounded
and rob the wagons. Perceiving this atrocity, Braddock
commanded Washington to rally the men who were
fleeing in every direction. By nightfall, retreat was the
only possibility. Though Washington had been on
horseback for more than twelve hours, Braddock

ordered him to guide the retreat. Moral courage was George Washington's solution to the physically impossible. After more than twenty-four consecutive hours of battle waged on horseback, on the morning of July 10, Washington's weary horse carried him to camp.

Braddock, in the meantime, was transported by cart, then transferred to a hand litter. When his spent men refused to carry him further, he mounted a horse and led the exhausted, frightened men back to camp. Braddock died on July 13, praising the gallantry and good conduct of his officers and deploring the bad behavior of the men.[35] Washington personally buried the British General with as much military dignity as the situation could afford. He made certain that no enemy Indians would discover the grave and desecrate the body of the fallen leader.

Later George Washington would say of his highly criticized deceased Commanding Officer:

"General Braddock was unfortunate, and his character was much too severely treated. He was one of the honestest and best men of the British officers with whom I was acquainted; even in manner of fighting he was not more to blame than others."[36]

George, as soon as his health improved, headed for his beloved Mount Vernon. He had overheard the laments of soldiers who believed they had been led into the wilderness to be slaughtered. The consensus of thinking men of the time was that General Braddock had been overconfident in an unfamiliar country where warfare was different in every way from what he knew and for which he was trained.

Subsequently, young Washington, in spite of or perhaps because of the legend of his excellence, was unjustly humiliated by his superiors in endeavors surrounding the Ohio Valley military campaign and the French and Indian War. This was a clear and painful purification for the brilliant young soldier.

George Washington's officers however, offered the following tribute to their twenty-six year old leader:

> "[H]e was the only man able to support 'the military character of Virginia', a chieftain who could by example 'inculcate those genuine sentiments of true honor and passion for glory from which the greatest military achievements have been derived.'"[37]

Washington remained in charge of Virginia's chain of border forts which protected colonists from Indian raids. He tamed the wilderness, recruited and trained militia, and garnered supplies and funds to support his troops. By 1758, London sent General John Forbes to conquer Fort Du Quesne and liberate the Western lands for the British crown. No longer a sick youth, but a tested warrior, Colonel Washington and his Virginia regiment had by November, moved to within a one day ride of Fort Du Quesne. They intended to camp there until Spring, when they would launch a full scale attack on the Fort and oust the French once and for all. Then, as luck would have it, a few prisoners fell into their hands, from whom they learned how weak and disabled the fortifications of the Fort actually were.

Wasting no time, Washington and his men achieved the victory he had so fervently prayed for in the back of the convoy wagon two years earlier. His joy was complete as he saluted the raising of the British flag at Fort Du Quesne. He wrote of the victory to Virginia Governor Francis Fauquier:

" I have the pleasure to inform you that Fort Du Quesne, or the ground rather on which it stood, was possessed by his Majesty's troops on the 25th instant. The enemy…burned the fort and ran away at night (by its light)."[38]

In 1758, believing his military career over, twenty-six year old Washington resigned his rank and retired to Mount Vernon. The officers who served with him were deeply disappointed and wrote to him: "In our earliest Infancy, you took us under your Tuition, train'd us up in the practice of that Discipline which alone can constitute good Troops."[39] They bewailed the "loss of such an excellent Commander, such a sincere friend, and so affable a companion."[40]

Washington now passed hours each day studying the Bible. Hunting was a favorite pastime. He also enjoyed learned conversation with his refined, affable neighbor George Mason. Washington frequently traveled by horseback through the vast untamed forests and wildernesses of Virginia, Maryland and Pennsylvania. Fifteen years after the great Battle of the Monongahela, Washington and a colleague were traveling through the Ohio Valley on a business trip. They were visited by an Indian tribe whose aged chief informed George—through an interpreter—that he had written a prophecy about Washington's life, and the nation he would found:

"I am chief and ruler over my tribes. My influence extends to the waters of the Great Lakes and to the far Blue Mountains. I have traveled a long and weary path, that I might see the young warrior of the great battle [George Washington at Fort Du Quesne]. It was on the day when the white man's blood mixed with the streams of our forest, that I first beheld this chief. I called to my young men and said, mark yon tall and daring warrior? He is not of the red-coat tribe—he hath an Indian's wisdom, and his warriors fight as we do—himself alone is exposed. Quick, let your aim be certain and he dies. Our rifles were leveled, rifles which, but for him, knew not how to miss—'twas all in vain, a power mightier far than we, shielded him from harm. He cannot die in battle. I am old, and soon shall be gathered to the great council fire of my fathers in the land of shades, but ere I go, there is something bids me speak in the voice of prophecy. Listen! The Great Spirit protects that man, and guides his destinies—he will become the chief of nations, and a people yet unborn will hail him as the founder of a mighty empire [of peace]."[41]

PART TWO

PART TWO

CHAPTER FOUR

Washington's Leadership

*"…[T]he ways of Providence are inscrutable, and
Mortals must submit."* [42]
—George Washington

Though he was a lifelong Christian, George Washington never imposed his personal faith on anyone. He respected everyone's faith as a sacred, God-given personal trust. During his Presidency, Washington wrote a memo to The Committee of Roman Catholics.

"…As mankind becomes more liberal, they will be more apt to allow that all those who conduct themselves as worthy members of the community [of whatever religious belief] are equally entitled to the protection of civil government. I hope ever to see America among the foremost nations in examples of justice and liberality."[43]

Washington wrote the following to the United Baptist Churches of Virginia:

"Every man, conducting himself as a good citizen and being accountable to God alone for his religious opinions, ought to be protected in worshipping the Deity according to the dictates of his conscience."[44]

Washington was convinced that religion and morality are the essential pillars of civil society, but he led by example, rarely by words. History is clear that Washington was keenly aware of his moral and religious duties. He intuitively knew that no man fully understands the mysterious ways of God. Throughout his life, Washington's personal relationship with Christ was intimately tied to his self-worth and self-esteem. He was uniquely renown throughout the world of his time as a humble man of God. Humility, a sign of man's relationship with God, was the uniform George Washington consistently chose. Humility is a characteristic of the soul. The more Washington grew in knowledge of Christ, the more humility became the fiber of his being.

Washington governed his actions by the principle that humility is not an external characteristic and therefore cannot be ascertained with the senses. Humility is a condition of the soul and no one can humanly judge the soul of another. The record is clear that in Washington's dealings with others, he held fast to the certitude that God alone is the just judge. He firmly believed and acted on the principle that one may discern a man's soul by his deeds.

Though History recounts little of Washington's childhood, family difficulties nourished seeds of leadership in Washington's character. Biographer Ferling observes:

"Nowhere in his vast correspondence does Washington reveal his feelings about his youth, other than to say that his parents sought to raise him so that he would never be 'in danger of becoming indolent ....imperious & dissipated'.[45]...After 1743, when George was on the cusp of adolescence, [his mother] lived alone with her children at Ferry Farm, a worn-out tract near Fredricksburg. Contemporaries describe her as quiet, aloof, imperious, and strong-willed.

She frightened some youngsters, who saw her as regal and omnipotent…It was in part from her that George likely derived his Olympian public persona of the quiet, stately, august individual…Washington's subsequent behavior suggests that he honored, and perhaps deeply loved, his mother."[46]

Washington enjoyed late teenage years with his half-brother Lawrence who… "associated with the most powerful men in the province and with the most sophisticated women that George had ever seen. Dashing, confident, polished, valorous, and not least the object of apparently heart-felt reverence and adulation, Lawrence was everything…"[47] George Washington however, as he reached early manhood, became the source of emotional and psychological support for Lawrence when he fell victim to tuberculoses. Helping his beloved elder brother, as he withered and died, was an experience in God's ways that George Washington's faith was powerful enough to withstand.

On July 3, 1775, when he took command of the Continental Army in dangerous and difficult circumstances, Washington's Army was the laughing stock of England. As Washington assumed command in the shade of an elm tree near the campus of Harvard College in Cambridge, Massachusetts, his men were poorly trained, poorly equipped and would rarely be paid. They were about to "...tangle with the largest expeditionary force sent forth in the eighteenth century."[48] There was, however, a mysterious promise of victory in the air that few could disregard. Three months earlier, young Patrick Henry had stood at the pulpit of Saint John's Church in Richmond, Virginia shouting

"Give me liberty or give me death!"
Those words were an electric current in the colonies that few understood at the time though all were seared by their power.

George Washington courageously shouldered the challenge of establishing America's freedom. He inaugurated the Herculean precedent that America's true spirit is sacrificial love, the only authentic love. True love gives life, breeds prosperity that sustains life and nourishes peace that ennobles life.

Washington was observed by others as a distinguished man who inspired admiration and commitment to nobler aspirations among his associates. One of his colleagues, Benjamin Latrobe remarked:

"There is something uncommonly commanding and majestic in his walk, his address, his figure and his countenance." [49]

An esteemed biographer said of him:

"Certainly Washington looked the part of Commander in Chief—almost six feet, four inches tall, and about two hundred pounds, athletic, and with the eye and bearing of a general." [50]

James Thomas Flexner said of Washington:

"...[F]rom the moment of his command, Washington was more than a military leader; he was the eagle, the standard, the flag, the living symbol of the cause." [51]

Another described Washington as a

"well mannered, quiet and impressive man with the military bearing...There was about him an aura of power, determination, dignity and probity that impressed everyone." [52]

Biographer James Thomas Flexner said of Washington:

"In all history, few men who possessed unassailable power have used that power so gently and self-effacingly for what their best instincts told them was the welfare of their neighbor and all mankind." [53]

Abigail Adams, wife of the Second President of the United States described Washington as being

"…[P]olite with dignity, affable without familiarity, distant without haughtiness, grave without austerity, modest, wise, and good."[54]

A biographer described George Washington in this way:

"Washington was no 'man of the people' to be clapped on the shoulder. In moments of seriousness his formality was severe and aristocratic—the product of a code developed under the old regime in Virginia. Yet he was a republican in the classic sense, and altogether in character when he declared: 'The approbation and affection of a free people [are] the greatest earthly rewards.'" [55]

Washington withstood adversity with as much dignity as his modesty allowed him to welcome success. On May 2, 1778, after the deprivation and desolation of the winter at Valley Forge, as Commander in Chief of the starving, pitiful revolutionary forces, General Washington encouraged his troops to ascend to the pinnacles of self-sacrifice for the good of others. He issued an order at Headquarters, Valley Forge, May 2, 1778, in which he asked them to consider the following:

"To the distinguished character of a Patriot it should be our highest glory to add the more distinguished character of a Christian."[56]

Washington was an icon of fortitude and fairness for his troops. His indomitable faith in the kindness of Divine Providence and the righteousness of America's cause are evident in historian Barbara W. Tuchman's description of the conditions he faced as Commander in Chief during the winter, 1779–1780 at Morristown, New Jersey.

"Rations were reduced for already hungry men who had been shivering in the snows to one-eighth of normal quantities. Two leaders of a protest by Connecticut regiments demanding full rations and back pay were hanged to quell an uprising. In January, 1781, Pennsylvania regiments mutinied and, with troops of New Jersey, deserted to the number of half their strength before the outbreak was suppressed. At the frontiers, Indians out of the woods guided by Loyalists were burning farms and massacring civilians. Even to keep an army in the field was problematical, because soldiers of the militia had to be furloughed to go home to harvest their crops, and if leave were refused, they would desert. Fighting a war in such circumstances, said General von Steuben, the army's Prussian drillmaster, 'Caesar and Hannibal would have lost their reputations.'"[57]

Washington loved his troops and asked much of them. He expected their lives, like his, to be poured out on behalf of their fellow citizens. He suffered with them, and triumphed with them. In April of 1778, Washington wrote the following to John Bannister about his troops.

"..[N]o Order of Men in the Thirteen States have paid a more sanctimonious regard to their proceedings than the Army; and, indeed it may be questioned, whether there has been that scrupulous adherence to them by any other, for without arrogance, or the smallest deviation from truth, it may be said that no history now extant can furnish an instance of an Army's suffering such uncommon hardships as ours have done, and bearing them with the same patience and Fortitude. To see men without clothes to cover their nakedness, without blankets to lay on, without shoes, by which their marches might be traced by the blood from their feet, and almost as often without provisions as with; marching through frost and snow, and at Christmas taking up their Winter Quarters within a day's march of the enemy, without a house or hut to cover them til they could be built, and submitting to it without a murmur, is a mark of patience and obedience which in my opinion can scarce be paralleled."[58]

Washington entwined love of country with the highest goals of the human character. He inspired citizens to the heights of sacrifice out of love for their country, for their families and for one another. He nourished the root of American patriotism with his belief that God creates human beings in His own image and likeness. Washington never wavered in his faith that God loves all His people and wills only the best for each.

Wisdom gave Washington eyes to see truth. Leaders great and small need that gift. He continuously experienced the earth as a testing ground. Wisdom unveiled many secrets to Washington: why humans exist, why God bothered to create humans, and what they are to do with their lives. Wisdom revealed that God sends humans to the earth to know Him as He allows, love Him as He deserves, serve Him as He desires, and to love and serve one another for Him, with Him and in Him. This reciprocity of love and service brings humans into union with God. George Washington's public life of leadership, his subsequent retirement at Mount Vernon, and the circumstances of his death disclose that he understood wisdom's imperative exquisitely.

George Washington embraced truth as his shield and his banner. After his death, Abigail Adams said of him:

"Simple truth is his best, his greatest eulogy. She alone can render his fame immortal."

George Washington was deeply aware of America's unique origin at the confluence of the tides of history and heroism.[59] His personal acuity, prayer life, commitment and discipline allowed him to receive and administer vast amounts of divine wisdom.[60] He was a man who valued principle above all else.[61] That resolution sustained Washington's visionary leadership in his personal life, on the battlefield and in public service.

Washington esteemed the inalienable rights of every human being of good will. He welcomed wisdom as his guide at the Constitutional Conventions. Wisdom pursued him in his deliberations as first President of the United States. Wisdom upheld him in his dedication to the responsibilities inherent in the ownership of private property. Wisdom carried him from the depths of sorrow to the heights of glory. Washington never took honor for himself. No true citizen does. Washington's wisdom reveals knowledge that life lived for a higher purpose than mere self is eternal.

Paradoxically, few men tasted more peace or exhibited more joy in it than the great warrior President. He was a peacemaker in the widest sense of the word. Washington believed that peace and joy find and dwell with those who are faithful to Christ's ways.

Washington prayed to know God's ways and respond fully. His men knew that about him; his faith was strong enough for all of them. Washington trusted that in God's Plan for humanity, all things, ideas, goals and achievements work together for peace. Peace on earth to men of good will is the birthright and endowment of the American way of life.

There is much wisdom to harvest now by an analysis of George Washington's spiritual life. Though certain Indians of Western Pennsylvania and even the less enlightened of his troops and constituencies may have perceived him as a god, Washington repudiated such claims and identified himself only as a servant of the Republic. His name was honored throughout America and in all the courts of Europe, yet he recognized himself only as a beloved beneficiary of God's mercy and a servant in the Kingdom of Love and just Peace.

America's Founding Father is not distinguished as a military genius. Yet he was. He is not esteemed as a landed aristocrat, though he was master of vast territory. Washington is not a literary giant, though his words dazzle the mind of every free person. Others claim such prizes, yet the spirit of George Washington hovers over America. Washington, always beloved as a citizen, an officer and a gentleman, is America's mystical icon of heroic grace. *U.S. News and World Report*, in a Special Collector's Edition published in September of 2002 reported:

"George Washington's character made him something of an exception to the dominant political style. He held more truly to the ideal of disinterested, principled, and nonpartisan leadership than any other founding brother. (Maybe, in his case, the sobriquet of father is just.) ..Although he could be stern, hot tempered, and unforgiving as deserters from the Continental Army learned with their lives, he was unfailingly a man of principle."[62]

George Washington cautioned against human hubris and that injunction remains as valid today as ever. He warned that those who seek glory for themselves are robbers. All honor, and glory and power belong to God our Father.

During his life on earth, Washington prayed and he prayed often. He prayed much that he might hear God's Voice. He prayed to know and remain faithful to God's ways. Now, the spirit of George Washington commissions this generation to respond to the graced Spirit of True Love. The Founding Father inspires us to pray fervently that we may hear God's Voice and follow Him to the Promised Land.

George Washington's prayer protects us as we bend and sway to the Presence of God in all that lives.

"I now make it my earnest prayer, that God would have you…in His holy protection, that He would incline the hearts of the citizens to cultivate a spirit of subordination and obedience to Government, to entertain a brotherly affection and love for one another, for their fellow citizens of the United States at large, and particularly for their brethren who have served in the Field [the military], and finally that He would most graciously be pleased to dispose us all to do Justice, to love mercy, and to demean ourselves with that Charity, humility and pacific temper of mind, which were the Characteristics of the Divine Author of our blessed Religion, and without an humble imitation of whose example in these things, we can never hope to be a happy Nation."[63]

In 1783, at a critical moment for the military and the Congress of the new nation, General Washington, whose faith in his troops and his country never wavered, grave and "agitated" according to an observer, stood before the victorious Continental army. Biographer Ferling describes the scene:

"Men hurried to their seats. Washington waited patiently until the scraping of chairs and all commotion ceased. When the room fell totally silent, he slowly unfolded a sheaf of papers, looked up one last time, then gazed at his notes and began to read. The men strained to hear him...He told the officers that he had been with them since the first, and that he had never left their side, save for times when Congress called him away. He spoke lovingly of the army, and of how his reputation was inextricably tied to it...He closed his prepared address by asking the officers to remember 'your sacred honor,' your country, the 'natural character of America,' and the 'rights of humanity.' He paused. Not a sound was heard in the great room. Slowly he reached again in his pocket. He extracted a pair of glasses, and slowly put them on. The men had never seen General Washington in spectacles...Looking over his glasses at the packed room, Washington begged their indulgence at his wearing glasses. In a soft voice that resonated with anger, fatigue, and unbridled despair, he told the officers: 'Gentlemen, you must pardon me. I have grown gray in your service and now find myself growing blind.' …Throughout the hall, men were weeping, tough men who had witnessed much carnage and had grown accustomed to life- and-death decisions…"[64]

Unquestionably, George Washington would always be their leader for sacrificial love knows no bounds.

George Washington knew the real meaning of life on earth.[65] His spirit invigorates all people. The America of our Founding Father is one nation under God with liberty and justice for all. Washington remains a reconciling force that can bring harmony to America, her allies and enemies alike.[66] Eventually good does triumph over evil in the life of mankind. Washington cautioned in his Circular to the States:

"…[T]he United States came into existence as a Nation, and if their citizens should not be completely happy, the fault will be entirely their own."

Washington promised that the pure and benign light of Revelation has a meliorating influence on mankind and increases the blessings of all.[67]

CHAPTER FIVE

Washington's Faith

"The time is now near at hand which must probably determine whether Americans are to be freemen or slaves; whether they are to have any property they can call their own: whether their houses and farms are to be pillaged and destroyed, and themselves consigned to a state of wretchedness from which no human efforts will deliver them. The fate of unborn millions will now depend, under God, on the courage and conduct of this army. Our cruel and unrelenting enemy leaves us only the choice of brave resistance, or the most abject submission. We have, therefore, to resolve to conquer or die."[68]

—General George Washington

*I*n 1776, George Washington led Americans to free-dom when hell opened its jaws to devour them and their property. He was not born a hero. He learned God's ways slowly. Freedom is expensive. It comes only from the Hand of God. True freedom from want of any kind is the goal of mankind. Freedom is always rooted in detachment from any person, place, thing, activity, ideal or goal contrary to God's loving plan for creation.

Washington understood that God's Son Jesus bought each soul with His own body and blood. His Scriptural disciplines showed him how to turn to God. Scripture showed Washington the proper use of his freedom on earth, which ends at biological death. He believed that true freedom is life in God. Consequently, for Washington, all that was not of God was deception. He found his path outlined in the Gospel. His mission was to become a faithful follower of Jesus Christ.

Duty forced George Washington to abstain from things and places of the world. His ways melted into God's will for the Lord gave him no other choices. Gradually, in prayer and Scripture he recognized God's Hand, he heard God's Voice. Graced discipline led him to the desert of obedience.

Young George liked to dance; he knew the courtly steps of Virginia's landed gentry. He had impeccable manners. He was handsome, elegant, gracious and witty. He savored fine food and appreciated excellent wine. He enjoyed the favor of high society and was comfortable in the finest salons of the times. He made himself at home in the wilderness. He was a friend and confidante of Indian leaders and frontiersmen. He always had to work. He witnessed much pain and endured immense anguish in his lifetime. He was not a fool. He knew that suffering would always be with us in the world. Aware that earth is a testing ground for the privileged, Washington was determined not to miss the time of God's visitation in his life.

The heights of asceticism beckoned to Washington constantly. As a youth, he had hoped to marry the daughter of a prosperous merchant in the Rappahannock Valley, but Betsy Fauntleroy rejected him. Washington quietly accepted this personal failure with peaceful resignation. Scarred by smallpox, as were many of his time, Washington had light blue eyes and brown hair. He was tall, especially for those times, lean and quite athletic. Leaders admired him. They "…discerned superior quality in him."[69] He was a popular youth who frequented social events of the Virginia gentry. George Washington very much enjoyed the company of beautiful, well-mannered ladies. He always appreciated goodness and admired virtue.

"History has canonized George Washington as the most esteemed of the Founding Fathers for many reasons. Without his transfiguring faith, personal self-sacrifice, expertise and, most significantly of all, victory on the battlefield, the Declaration of Independence would have been a seal of defeat and certain death for the signers."

5   "As Washington assumed command...near the campus of Harvard College in Cambridge, Massachusetts, his men were poorly trained, poorly equipped and would rarely be paid. They about to '...tangle with the largest expeditionary force sent forth in the eighteenth century.'

6   "Washington...said that his triumphs at Trenton and Princeton proceeded from good fortun
He knew that fortune favors the brave and the bold.
He also knew, adored, and obeyed the Divine Source of good fortune."

In spite of his charm and obvious social nature, Washington was a deeply spiritual man. The prism of history shows us the depth of Washington's trust in the love and providential hand of God in his life. He was forthright in his belief that God guides human history. Washington was a dedicated, lifelong student of Biblical revelation. It is recorded:

> "During his residence in Philadelphia, as President of the United States, it was the habit of Washington, winter and summer, to retire to his study at a certain hour every night. He usually did so at nine o'clock...A youthful member of the household whose room was near the study saw him [Washington] upon his knees at a small table, with a candle and open Bible thereon."[70]

Throughout his life, Washington assiduously avoided false and pretentious piety. He had little time for foolish myth. He disavowed superstition. This practical characteristic ennobled him to his colleagues and foes alike. Washington relied on the Scriptural promises of a God whose Heart is filled with love for His poor, sinful children. He trusted Christ as the Savior of the world, the Prince of Peace, the Source of freedom on earth. Washington, all too often called to forgo his own comfort and pleasure, lived as if there is no tomorrow for anyone. Rather, as he would remind his troops, his colleagues and family, there is only and always the Eternal Now. Life experience taught him that lesson from an early age.

Washington's personal sense of freedom and self-worth rested in his relationship with God. In early 1799, the year of his death, he wrote of himself to Bryan Fairfax:

> "The favorable sentiments which others, you say, have been pleased to express respecting me, cannot but be pleasing to a mind (sic) who always walked on a straight line, and endeavored as far as human frailties, and perhaps strong passions, would enable him, to discharge the relative duties to his Maker and fellow-men, without seeking any indirect or left handed attempts to acquire popularity."[71]

Washington actively sought to know God's will for him, and he prayed fervently to obey God's ways. Though Washington was a man who cherished above all else the peace and comfort of home and family, circumstances raised him up to be a great warrior. He drank deep of the bitter cup of defeat. He remained lowly though he was six feet four inches tall without his boots and attained to the heights of national leadership. He was widely known to be humble and modest. Washington remained silent as much as possible. He always strove to bring discipline, humor, beauty, courtesy, bounty and prosperity to his family, his fellow citizens, his beloved Mount Vernon, his troops,[72] the city of Alexandria, the Capital, schools, Universities, the width and breadth of the new nation.[73]

Chief Justice John Marshall, in his contemporary biography of the First President of the United States noted the path of freedom that Washington traveled:

"Endowed by nature with a sound judgment, and an accurate and discriminating mind, he feared not that laborious attention which made him perfectly master of those subjects, in all their relations, on which he was to decide; and this essential quality was guided by an unvarying sense of moral right, which would tolerate the employment only of those means that would bear the most rigid examination; by a fairness of intention which neither sought nor required disguise; and by a purity of virtue which not only was untainted, but unsuspected."[74]

Washington's early military career forced him to deal with the savagery of Indian raiders against Colonial settlers, and such debauchery seared his soul, making him a total realist. He was perceptive of treachery, especially among those unaware of the mercy of God's redeeming love. On October 25, 1755, settlement families near Wills Creek were severely victimized in a classic Cain and Abel conflict. Washington saw the unburied bodies of a scalped woman, a small boy and a young man near their burned out farmhouse. His soldiers found three people brained with stakes, scalped and thrown into a fire that only half consumed them. Washington determined that adequate security for settlers who had rightful title to their property was of absolute necessity. He also realized that "Indians are the only match for Indians."[75] Washington therefore created alliances with friendly Indians that would protect property rights of landowners.

Washington's burning faith in his youth, during his military career, throughout his presidency and retirement solidified American political, religious, financial and personal freedom, and that freedom has flourished for more than two hundred years. He had a keen sense of the mysterious connection between religious freedom and financial prosperity. He personally experienced the connection between financial prosperity and personal freedom. Washington gives us a brilliant legacy of religious kindliness that goes far beyond condescending tolerance. Wisdom speaks in Washington's commands regarding Roman Catholicism[76] in Quebec where certain troops were being deployed.

> "…[A]void all disrespect to or contempt of the Religion of the Country and its ceremonies. Prudence, Policy and a true Christian Spirit will lead us to look with compassion upon the[m]…without insulting them. While we are contending for our own Liberty, we should be very cautions of violating the Rights of Conscience in others, ever considering that God alone is the Judge of the Hearts of Men, and to Him only in this case, they are answerable."[77]

Washington and those he led forged a life of personal freedom and prosperity on the North American continent unique in the world's history. George Washington's spiritual strength stands guard over every person's moral obligation to seek above all "the pure and benign light of Revelation" to make the world "a display of human greatness and felicity."[78]

In modern times, dark forces of savagery have perpetrated deliberate and massive atrocity against lawful inhabitants of private property. Such aberrant behavior requires people of all nations to take a stand for peace and liberty under just law. Peace will come, but at a price that few willingly pay.

Washington saw much terrorism firsthand, of course on a smaller but no less violent scale, in the wilderness on the frontier. He learned from the Bible the art of dealing with uncertain terrorists. In Washington's lifetime, just government depended on moral Indians and white men for the defense of the frontiers. One of his allies was the powerful Indian leader "Half King."

Early in his military career, when young Major Washington met Half King, he described this man as

"...intelligent, vain, brave, as candid as an Indian ever was, and possessed of an unusual knowledge of white men and their method of fighting. When his passion was stirred, Half King would assert that the reason he hated the French was that they had killed, boiled and eaten his father. More immediately he had a bitter grudge because of treatment he had recently had...."[79]

Washington befriended the outraged Indian leader and learned much from him.

George Washington's diplomatic style was to remain sober at all times and listen intently.[80] His divine calling was to salvage and nurture the alliance of decent people of good will for the common good. In the French, English and Indian conflict over the Ohio Valley, and later during the Revolutionary War, the Constitutional Conventions, his Presidency and retirement, Washington adhered assiduously to his faith beliefs.

Since Bunker Hill, self-sacrifice has been the American way. During his frontier command, Washington wrote his superior:

> "I shall be studious to avoid all disputes that may tend to the public prejudice, but as far as I am able, I will inculcate harmony and unanimity."[81]

Contemporary Americans know how to follow the Golden Rule. They take to the streets to give blood, bring food, clothing, medical aid and moral support in time of need. Americans rally to give what they have so that others might live and experience love. In every moment of infamy, people of good will are one. There are no strangers at the foot of the cross. Suffering introduces us to our lofty origin.

Faithful commitment to daily duty makes Americans targets for a new kind of warfare, hideous in its sleuth, deceit and monstrosity. Americans who die at their posts to defend freedom do not die in vain. God always brings good out of evil. Their sacrifice on the frontier of liberty unmasks segments of the world inhabited by lost souls wallowing in the darkness of revolution, steeped in greed, selfishness, avarice, envy, lust and hatred. The perpetrators send their executioners to the four winds but they will not prevail. They never have in the past, not since Cain killed Abel. Washington's spirit reaches through the centuries to remind every freedom loving person of the sacred duty to route evil from the planet.

Freedom from terror is expensive. The price is not negotiable. As in the past, so now lives, fortunes and the sacred honor of every peace loving human being are on the line to preserve liberty under just law. America's national moral character manifests itself in self-sacrifice. Many have died helping their fallen brothers and sisters. It has always been so in America. No one has greater love than to lay down his or her life for another. America will overcome adversity.

People of good will live an eternal commitment to one another. The dignity of history guides us now as we struggle to become a global family. All people of good conscience hear the call. Though America and her allies are the moral frontier today, tomorrow is drenched in Liberty's Light.

Sacrifice is the food of heroes. Liberty under morally just law is not an easy way of life. Frontiers are like that. George Washington brilliantly perceived that if American ideals are to remain a light for the world, our unity as a people of God is our uniform of honor. Liberty under just law is the only life. Washington wrote to the Hebrew Congregation of Newport, Rhode Island, on September 9, 1790.

"The citizens of the United States of America have a right to applaud themselves for having given to mankind…a policy worthy of imitation. All possess alike liberty of conscience, and immunities of citizenship. It is now no more that toleration is spoken of, as if it was by the indulgence of one class of people, that another enjoyed the exercise of their inherent natural rights. For happily the government of the United States, which gives to bigotry no sanction—to persecution no assistance, requires only that they who live under its protection should demean themselves as good citizens, in giving it on all occasions their effectual support."[82]

Washington never wavered in his belief that all blessings, benefits and prosperity flow from the Divine Hand of God. Desiring only the best for good citizens, he firmly enjoined moral righteousness as a nonnegotiable requirement for everyone when He wrote to the Presbyterian Church General Assembly on May 26, 1789:

"While I reiterate the professions of my dependence upon Heaven as the source of all public and private blessings; I will observe that the general prevalence of piety, philanthropy, honesty, industry, and economy seems, in the ordinary course of human affairs, particularly necessary for advancing and confirming the happiness of our country. While all men within our territories are protected in worshipping the Deity according to the dictates of their consciences; it is rationally to be expected from them in return, that they will be emulous of evincing the sanctity of their professions by the innocence of their lives and the beneficence of their actions; for no man, who is profligate in his morals, or a bad member of the civil community, can possibly be a true Christian, or a credit to his own religious society."[83]

George Washington could be trusted with power. He recognized himself and others simply as unworthy servants of the great God of Abraham. He believed that obedience to God brings blessings of peace and prosperity, which must be earned. He wrote:

> "The man must be bad indeed who can look upon the events of the American Revolution without feeling the warmest gratitude towards the great Author of the Universe whose divine interposition was so frequently manifested on our behalf. And it is my earnest prayer that we may so conduct ourselves as to merit a continuance of those blessings with which we have hitherto been favored."[84]

At the Battle of Princeton, as was his custom during the Revolutionary War, Washington

> "...[P]referred to risk his own life to achieve success rather than to remain safely behind his men and perhaps in consequence to receive reports of defeat. Conspicuous on a white horse,

he rode forward within thirty yards of the British line, urging the men of Mercer and Cadwalader to follow him in attack. The smoke of gunfire enveloped him. His men feared that he was slain, but he was unscathed. The Patriots rallied behind him."[85]

Washington later said that his triumphs at Trenton and Princeton proceeded from good fortune. He knew that fortune favors the brave and the bold.[86] He also knew, adored and obeyed the Divine Source of good fortune. When his troops were weak from lack of food at Valley Forge, barefooted and persecuted by the bitter cold, art history records that their Commander-in Chief faced that hardship on his knees in the snow. Such is the hero tradition he bequeaths to people of good will.

In Washington's era, Americans believed in God. Contemporaries rightfully grapple with the benevolence of Divine Providence evident in Washington's life and times. Consider the following:

"His [Washington's] physical appearance was complemented by an aura, not merely of strength, but of invincibility. His immunity to gunfire seemed almost supernatural. Early in his career a treacherous guide fired at him from point-blank range—and missed. Once he rode between two columns of his own men who were firing at one another by mistake and struck up their guns with his sword—the musket balls whizzed harmlessly by his head. Time and time again during the Revolutionary War musket balls tore his clothes, knocked off his hat, and shredded his cape; horses were killed under him; but he was never touched. What mortal could refuse to entrust his life to a man whom God obviously favored? What country could refuse to do so?"[87]

Washington's life and accomplishments are models of wisdom's compassion that guides the work of all true great leaders. Washington's lived faith in the power of God's love to spawn human freedom is a luminescent torch of hope for people of good will in the twenty-first century.

Washington's courage was horrendously assailed in battle, yet he never wavered. At the political formation of the government of the United States, his prayerful leadership, wielded for the most part in silent observance, engendered courageous vision among his colleagues. His steadfast humility throughout two terms as first President of a unique infant nation breathed life into government for the people, by the people and of the people. Washington consistently led by example and rarely by word. His sacrificial, largely hidden service in retirement shored up a fledgling nation struggling to become "the City [of God] on the Hill."

Today, in contemporary light, Washington's enduring faith illumines the astonishing financial, political and diplomatic achievements of the American form of government. Washington's principled leadership flowed from his understanding of the Bible. His social/spiritual ideology charted the course for America's soul-wrenching journey into the morning light of God's freedom.

CHAPTER SIX

The Declaration of Independence

*W*hen in the Course of human events, it becomes necessary for one people to dissolve the political bands which have connected them with another, and to assume among the powers of the earth, the separate and equal station to which the Laws of Nature and Nature's God entitle them, a decent respect to the opinions of mankind requires that they should declare the causes which impel them to the separation.—

We hold these truths to be self evident, that all men are created equal, that they are endowed by their Creator with certain unalienable Rights, that among these are Life, Liberty and the pursuit of Happiness.—

That to secure these rights, Governments are instituted among Men, deriving their just powers from the consent of the governed.—

That whenever any Form of Government becomes destructive of these ends, it is the Right of the People to alter or to abolish it, and to institute new Government, laying its foundation on such principles and organizing its powers in such form, as to them shall seem most likely to effect their Safety and Happiness. Prudence, indeed, will dictate that Governments long established should not be changed for light and transient causes; and accordingly all experience hath shewn, that man-kind are more disposed to suffer, while evils are sufferable, than to right themselves by abolishing the forms to which they are accustomed. But when a long train of abuses and usurpations, pursuing invariably the same Object evinces a design to reduce them under absolute Despotism, it is their right, their duty, to throw off such Government, and to provide new Guards for their future security.—

Such has been the patient suffering of these Colonies; and such is now the necessity which constrains them to alter their former Systems of Government. The history of the present King of Great Britain is a history of repeated injuries and usurpations, all having in direct object the establishment of an absolute Tyranny over these States. To prove this, let facts be submitted to a candid world.—

He has refused his Assent to Laws, the most wholesome and necessary for the public good.—

He has forbidden his Governors to pass Laws of immediate and pressing importance, unless suspended in their operation till his Assent should be obtained; and when so suspended, he has utterly neglected to attend to them.—

He has refused to pass other Laws for the accommodation of large districts of people, unless those people would relinquish the right of representation in the Legislature, a right inestimable to them and formidable to tyrants only.—

He has called together legislative bodies at places unusual, uncomfortable, and distant from the depository of their public Records, for the sole purpose of fatiguing them into compliance with his measures.—

He has dissolved Representative Houses repeatedly, for opposing with manly firmness his invasions on the rights of the people.—

He has refused for a long time, after such dissolutions, to cause others to be elected; whereby the Legislative powers, incapable of Annihilation, have returned to the People at large for their exercise; the State remaining in the mean time exposed to all the dangers of invasion from without, and convulsions within.—

He has endeavored to prevent the population of these States; for that purpose obstructing the Laws for Naturalization of Foreigners; refusing to pass others to encourage their migrations hither, and raising the conditions of new Appropriations of Lands.—

He has obstructed the Administration of Justice, by refusing his Assent to Laws for establishing Judiciary powers.—

He has made Judges dependent on his will alone, for the tenure of their offices, and the amount and payment of their salaries.—

He has erected a multitude of New Offices, and sent hither swarms of Officers to harass our people, and eat out their substance.—

He has kept among us, in times of peace, Standing Armies without the consent of our legislatures.—

He has effected to render the Military independent of and superior to the Civil power.—

He has combined with others to subject us to a jurisdiction foreign to our constitution, and acknowledged by our laws; giving his Assent to their Acts of pretended Legislation.—

For quartering large bodies of armed troops among us.—

For protecting them, by a mock Trial, from punishment for any Murders which they should commit on the Inhabitants of these States.—

For cutting off our Trade with all parts of the world: —

For imposing Taxes on us without our Consent:—

For depriving us in many cases, of the benefits of Trial by Jury:—

For transporting us beyond Seas to be tried for pretended offenses:—

For abolishing the free System of English Laws in a neighboring Province, establishing therein an Arbitrary government, and enlarging its Boundaries so as to render it at once an example and fit instrument for introducing the same absolute rule into these Colonies:—

For taking away our Charters, abolishing our most valuable laws, and altering fundamentally the Forms of our Governments:—

For suspending our own Legislatures, and declaring themselves invested with power to legislate for us in all cases whatsoever.—

He has abdicated Government here, by declaring us out of his Protection and waging War against us.—

He has plundered our seas, ravaged our Coasts, burnt our towns, and destroyed the lives of our people.—

He is at this time transporting large Armies of foreign Mercenaries to complete the works of death, desolation and tyranny, already begun with circumstances of Cruelty and perfidy scarcely paralleled in the most barbarous ages, and totally unworthy the Head of a civilized nation.—

He has constrained our fellow Citizens taken captive on the high Seas to bear Arms against their Country, to become the executioners of their friends and Brethren, or to fall themselves by their Hands.—

He has incited domestic insurrections amongst us, and has endeavored to bring on the inhabitants of our frontiers, the merciless Indian Savages, whose known rule of warfare, is an undistinguished destruction, of all ages, sexes and conditions.

In every stage of these Oppressions We have Petitioned for Redress in the most humble terms: Our repeated Petitions have been answered only by repeated injury. A prince, whose character is thus marked by every act which may define a Tyrant, is unfit to be the ruler of a free people.

Nor have we been wanting in attentions to our British brethren. We have warned them from time to time of attempts by their legislature to extend an unwarrantable jurisdiction over us. We have reminded them of the circumstances of our emigration and settlement here. We have appealed to their native justice and magnanimity, and we have conjured them by the ties of our common kindred to disavow these usurpation's, which, would inevitably interrupt our connections and correspondence. They too have been deaf to the voice of justice and consanguinity. We must, therefore, acquiesce in the necessity, which denounces our Separation, and hold them, as we hold the rest of mankind, Enemies in War, in Peace Friends.—

We, therefore, the Representatives of the United States of America, in General Congress, Assembled, appealing to the Supreme Judge of the world for the rectitude of our intentions, do, in the Name, and by Authority of the good People of these Colonies, solemnly publish and declare, That these United Colonies are, and of Right ought to be Free and Independent States; that they are Absolved from all Allegiance to the British Crown, and that all political connection between them and the State of Great Britain, is and ought to be totally dissolved; and that as Free and Independent States, they have full Power to levy War, conclude Peace, contract Alliances, establish Commerce, and do all other Acts and Things which Independent States may of right do.—

And for the support of this Declaration, with a firm reliance on the protection of divine Providence, we mutually pledge to each other our Lives, our Fortunes, and our sacred Honor.

PART THREE

PART THREE

CHAPTER SEVEN

In Defense of Freedom

"…I shall never suffer private convenience to
interfere with what I conceive to be
my official duties."[88]
—*George Washington*

By 1774, George Washington, representing Virginia, was a member of the Continental Congress that assembled at Philadelphia in the month of September. Unfortunately, a self-appointed vigilante committee, The Association had commissioned themselves to oversee the daily activities of Americans under the guise of 'encouraging frugality, economy and industry, …..discontinuance of every species of extravagance and dissipation, especially all horse racing, and all kinds of gaming, cock-fighting, exhibitions of shews, plays and other expensive diversions and entertainments.' Though ill-advised members of the committee hoped the Association would bring speedy concessions from the British Parliament, it did not. A rather lawless state of affairs exacerbated a fire keg mentality among the colonists. The Continental Congress then drafted a Declaration of Rights and Grievances, along with a plenary petition to the King of England.

The Continental Congress ended but not before misunderstandings between the British monarchy and the colonists exploded. The Revolutionary War began on the night of April 18, 1775, at Lexington, Massachusetts. Colonists quickly circulated the news that the King's forces had maliciously and wantonly opened fire, killing innocent, peaceful villagers. Of course, the story is not that simple. Nevertheless, eight minute-men, as the patriot warriors were called, lay dead in the village square in the early morning light. On marched the British forces to Concord where the 'shot that was heard round the world' was fired. Then the British marched to Boston, but not before the death or maiming of 247 British red coats.

The second Continental Congress assembled in Philadelphia shortly thereafter on May 10, and a highly distinguished group it was. Though hopeful for conciliation with Great Britain, the mood of the men present was ominous. Each believed his cause was just, the Union a necessity. No one doubted God's will for the preservation of their liberties, being with one mind resolved to die free men rather than live as slaves.[89]

By 23 June, 1776, it became clear that war with England was inevitable. George Washington, the most esteemed military leader among the Founders was appointed Commander in Chief of the American forces. Though he did not desire the post, his patriotism and high moral sense of stewardship left him no choice but to serve. He was quite obviously aware of the danger he was undertaking. One of his first acts after the appointment was to draft a new Last Will and Testament, so as to provide for his wife, her children, their staff, employees, workers and slaves. He refused a salary for his services but asked the Congress to cover his expenses.[90] As the new Commander in Chief departed Philadelphia, a messenger met him along the road bringing devastating news of the Battle of Bunker Hill.

Riding into battle with an ill-equipped, poorly trained militia comprised of farmers, fishermen and merchants, General Washington was aware that much of the world lives in darkness.[91] His vision of the times was bathed in the hopes of those who seek to live in the Light.[92] This gentleman of the wilderness knew the voice of His maker deep in his soul.[93] He sincerely believed the American cause was just.[94] George Washington desired simply to serve God and the new nation.[95]

General Washington recognized he would bear personal responsibility for America's victory or defeat. He wrote:

> "...[F]ar from seeking this appointment (as Commander in Chief), I have used every endeavor in my power to avoid it...from the consciousness of its being a trust too great for my capacity.[96]

Washington addressed the horror of Bunker Hill with hope that soon Americans would be free to fully adhere to God's Scriptural ways. Battle seemed the only alternative in those days and Washington resigned himself to the call of duty. He and his troops would henceforth be required to deliver the colonists from the tyrannical oppressors on their shores. Warrior that his fate called him to be, Washington would pray and work and die for all to live peacefully.

By winter of 1777, Washington's courage and bravery were sorely tested. His soldiers were ragged. They were hungry—even starving. They had nothing to keep them warm that bitter winter except the fire of love in their hearts for their families and the infant nation they struggled to cherish. These brave visionaries faced inhuman odds as the hardships of Valley Forge loomed on the horizon.[97] Then their faith filled Commander in chief, in full view of his troops, knelt in the snow to implore the blessings and providence of Almighty God on the dedicated men who carried the hopes and dreams of freedom in their hearts.

God sometimes answers prayers in supernatural ways we least expect. During those dark days of starvation and defeat at Valley Forge, an extraordinary spiritual event occurred sometime between 18 and 23 December.[98] A mysterious and unidentified "Beautiful Woman from Heaven" appeared to console, inspire and guide the needy General Washington.[99] One can only hypothesize who that being of celestial splendor might have been. Perhaps it was the Guardian Angel of the United States.[100]

The Beautiful Woman may have been Mary, the Mother of Jesus Christ, the Biblical Woman of Genesis 3:15. An explanation for that possibility rests in Washington's knowledge of Catholicism. His faithful friend, business partner and confidante, Daniel Carroll who signed the Declaration of Independence on behalf of the State of Maryland was a devout Catholic. His younger brother John Carroll studied for the priesthood at a Jesuit seminary in Liege, France. After enduring severe religious persecution in France, he returned to Maryland in 1774. Subsequently, John Carroll became the first Catholic Archbishop of the American Colonies. He most likely would have been aware of the mystical phenomenon General Washington experienced at Valley Forge for three reasons.

(1) The Washington and Carroll families were quite close.[101] On June 11, 1799, six months before General Washington's death, Archbishop John Carroll conferred and dined with Washington at Mount Vernon. When he founded Georgetown University, Carroll insisted the University never become a "Catholic Ghetto....When Georgetown was opened as a seat of learning, the President's house [White House] was not yet built in Washington. The cornerstone was laid by the free masons in 1792. General Washington was present."[102]

(2) The Catholic Church, both Roman and Anglican share a long history of Marian apparitions, especially in times of danger and sorrow.

(3) George Washington was an astute man who consistently sought advice about matters outside his own frame of reference. John Carroll would have been an expert by training about Marian apparitions.

In his official capacity as First Catholic Archbishop of the United States, John Carroll, in 1792, solemnly and permanently entrusted the new nation and it's citizens to the Lord Jesus Christ through Mary, His Mother. Washington of course would have known of this sacred consecration and its consequences. He may have participated personally. The text of the official consecration of the United States to Mary follows.

Consecration of the United States of America to Mary

Most Holy Trinity, Our Father in Heaven,
Who chose Mary as the fairest of Your daughters;
Holy Spirit Who chose Mary as Your Spouse;
God the Son Who chose Mary as Your Mother,

In union with Mary, we adore Your Majesty

And acknowledge Your supreme, eternal dominion and authority.

Most Holy Trinity, we place the United States of America

Into the hands of Mary Immaculate

In order that she may present the country

To You.

Through her we wish to thank You for the great resources of this land

And for the freedom which has been its heritage.

Through the intercession of Mary, have mercy on the Catholic Church in America.

Grant us peace.

Have mercy on our President

And on all the officers of our government.

Grant us a fruitful economy, born of justice and labor.

Protect the family life of the nation.

Guard the precious gift of many religious vocations.

Through the intercession of Mary Our Mother, have mercy on the sick,

The tempted, sinners...on all who are in need.

Mary, Immaculate Virgin, Our Mother,
Patroness of our land, we praise and honor you
And give ourselves to you.
Protect us from every harm.
Pray for us, that acting always according to your will
And the will of your Divine Son,
We may live and die pleasing to God. Amen.[103]
   —John Carroll, 1792

There is historical precedent for the possibility that it truly was the Blessed Mother whom General Washington saw that bleak day at Valley Forge.[104] Through Mary, "the Mosaic Law arrived at the threshold of its fulfillment, and God's promise to the world and covenant with Abraham was fulfilled: 'God promised Abraham the forefather that in his seed shall the nations be blessed...And through [Mary] the promise comes to pass...'"[105] It is understood: "All who have known God from the beginning and have foretold the coming of Christ have received the revelation from the Son Himself."[106]

George Washington, the Commander in Chief of the American cause had great need of divine intervention on behalf of his highly distressed troops at Valley Forge. God has historically sent the Blessed Mother

Mary as His ambassador of Divine Mercy, Comfort of the Afflicted in times of great human need.[107]

An eyewitness of George Washington's testimony concerning his celestial vision, Anthony Sherman later recounted segments of the heavenly phenomenon to Wesley Bradshaw. The oral history of this apparition to the American Commander in Chief at Valley Forge was originally published in *The National Tribune*, Volume 4, No. 12, December 1880, and is preserved in the Library of Congress in Washington, DC.[108]

"George Washington was not a [Roman] Catholic. Even if he had been he would hardly have been the type of man one would expect to be seeking visionary manifestations, or easily be taken in by them. From the opening of the (American) Revolution we experienced all phases of fortune, now good and now ill, one time victorious and another time conquered. The darkest period we had, I think, was when Washington, after several reverses, retreated to Valley Forge, where he resolved to pass the winter of 1777. Ah! I have often seen the tears course down our dear commander's careworn cheeks, as he would be conversing with confidential officers about the condition of his poor soldiers. You have doubtless heard the story of Washington going to the thicket to pray. It was not only true but he used often to pray in secret for aid and comfort from God, the Interposition of whose Divine Providence brought us safely through the darkest days of tribulation."

"One day, I remember it well, the chilly wind whistled through the leafless trees, though the sky was cloudless and the sun shone brightly. He remained in his quarters nearly all afternoon alone. When he came out I noticed that his face was a shade paler than usual, and there seemed to be something on his mind of more than ordinary importance. Returning just after dark, he dispatched an orderly to the quarters of another officer, who was presently in attendance. After a preliminary conversation of about half an hour, Washington, gazing upon us with that strange look of dignity, which he alone could command, said:

"I do not know whether it is owing to the anxiety of my mind, but this afternoon, as I was sit-ing at this table engaged in preparing a dispatch, something disturbed me. Looking up, I saw standing opposite a singularly beautiful female. So astonished was I, for I had given strict orders not to be disturbed, that it was some moments before I found language to inquire the purpose of her presence. A second, third, even a fourth time did I repeat my question but received no answer from my mysterious visitor, except a slight raising of her eyes. By this time I felt strange sensations spreading through me. I would have risen but the riveted gaze of the being before me rendered volition impossible. I essayed once more to address her, but my tongue had become useless. Even thought itself had become paralyzed. A new influence, mysterious, potent, irresistible, took possession of me. All I could do was to gaze steadily, at my unknown visitor. Gradually the surrounding atmosphere filled with sensation and grew luminous. Everything about me seemed to rarefy, the mysterious visitor herself becoming more airy and yet more distinct to my sight than before. I now began to feel as one dying, or rather to experience the sensation which I have sometimes imagined accompanies dissolution. I did not think, I did not reason, I did not move. All, alike, were impossible. I was conscious only of gazing fixedly at my companion.

Presently I heard a voice say, "Son of the Republic, look and learn! while at the same time my visitor extended her arm eastward. I looked and beheld a heavy white vapor rising, at some distance, fold upon fold. This gradually dissipated and I watched before me lay spread out in one vast plain all the countries of the world: Europe, Asia, Africa and America. I saw rolling and tossing between Europe and America, the billows of the Atlantic Ocean, and between America and Asia lay the Pacific.

"Son of the Republic" said the mysterious voice as before, "look and learn." "At that moment I beheld a dark shadowy being, standing, or rather floating in mid-air between Europe and America. Dipping water out of the ocean with his right hand, he cast it upon America, while that in his left hand went upon the European countries. Immediately a cloud arose from these countries, and joined in mid-ocean. For awhile it remained stationery, and then it moved slowly westward, until it enveloped America in its folds. Sharp flashes of lighting gleamed through at intervals; and I heard the smothered groans of the American people. A second time the angel dipped water from the ocean and sprinkled it as before. The dark cloud was then drawn back to the ocean, in whose heaving bellows it sank from view.

A third time I heard the mysterious voice say: "Son of the Republic, look and learn." "I cast my eyes upon America and beheld villages, towns and cities springing up one after another until the whole land, from the Atlantic to the Pacific, was dotted with them.

Again I heard the voice say, "Son of the Republic, the end of the century comes. Look and learn." And with this the dark, shadowy angel turned its face southward, and from Africa an ill-omened spectra approached our land. It flitted slowly over every town and city of the land. The inhabitants presently set themselves in battle array against each other.

"As I continued to look I saw a bright angel, on whose brow rested a crown of light on which was traced the word UNION, place an American flag between the divided nation and say: "Remember ye are brethren." Instantly the inhabitants, casting from them weapons, became friends once more and united around the National Standard.

"Again I heard the voice of my most beautiful and mysterious visitor say, 'Son of the Republic, look and learn.' At this, the dark, shadowy angel placed a trumpet to his mouth and blew three distinct blasts; and taking water from the ocean he sprinkled it upon Europe, Asia and Africa.

"Then my eyes beheld a fearful scene: from each of these countries arose thick black clouds that were soon joined into one. Throughout this mass there gleamed a bright Red Light, by which I saw hordes of armed men, who, moving with the cloud, marched by land and sailed by sea to America which country was enveloped in the volume of cloud.

"And I saw these vast armies devastate the whole country and burn the villages, towns and cities that I saw springing up. As my ears listened to the thundering of the canon, the clashing of the swords, and the shouts and cries of millions in mortal combat, I again heard the mysterious voice say: 'Son of the Republic, look and learn.'

"As the voice ceased, the bright angel, for the last time, dipped water from the ocean and sprinkled it upon America. Instantly the dark cloud rolled back, together with the armies it had brought, leaving the inhabitants of the land victorious. Once more I beheld villages, towns and cities springing up where I had seen them before; while the bright angel, planting the azure standard he had brought in the middle of them, cried in a loud voice, 'While the stars remain and the heavens send down dew upon the earth, so long shall the Union last'.

"And taking from her angelic brow the crown on which was blazoned the word UNION, she placed it upon the National Standard, while people kneeling down, said, 'Amen'.

"The scene instantly began to fade away, and I saw nothing but the rising, curling vapor I had first beheld. This also disappeared and I found myself once more gazing upon the mysterious beautiful visitor who said, 'Son of the Republic what you have seen is thus: three great perils will come upon the Republic. The most fearful is the third, but the whole world united shall not prevail upon her. Let every child of the Republic learn to live for God, his land and the Union.' With these words the beautiful visitor and the bright angel accompanying her disappeared from my sight."

"Such, my friend, were the very words I heard from Washington's own lips and America will do well to profit by them." concluded the narrator of this Oral History.[109]

Modern philosophers observe various historical possibilities in the scenes that General Washington observed. Perhaps the most challenging is the third vision. One can hope it has nothing to do with the current war of terrorism that scourges America. If however, such is the case, committed faithfulness to daily duty promises enduring peace so long as we stand united, learning to live for God, our land and the Union.

Following General Washington's spiritual experience at Valley Forge, the tide of victory for the United States turned. Prussian military expert Baron Von Steuben made a commitment to train the American militia at Valley Forge and the French decided to becomes allies of the new nation.

Victory for the United States was far from easy. Immense darkness enveloped the American cause by the early months of 1781. Washington was put to further spiritual tests as he endured his own "agony in the garden." Was this war, and his role in it really God's plan? he pondered. And if so, did he truly trust God's power, in spite of the obvious poverty and inadequacy of his troops?[110]

Washington had a pitiful army, even after the best efforts of General Von Steuben. The fact that the continental currency was often worthless allowed the States to refuse to honor requisitions for even the most basic needs of the Revolutionary Forces. A Pennsylvania regiment, overcome by the lack of clothing and food actually mutinied.

Washington prayed. Quite correctly, he realized that no victory would be possible without superior sea power. He wrote an urgent message to French General Rochambeau who had six thousand men sequestered at Newport, Rhode Island, pleading for quick and decisive help:

> "In any operation, and under all circumstances, a decisive naval superiority is to be considered a fundamental principle, and the basis upon which every hope of success must ultimately depend."[111]

Simultaneously, Washington dispatched a special envoy to King Louis XVI in Paris with his pressing request for immediate naval assistance. Washington prevailed. Through the masterful diplomatic skills of Benjamin Franklin, France entered the American Revolution on the side of the colonists.

French naval help was quick, powerful and decisive. Admiral Compte de Grasse was dispatched to the rescue and sailed from Haiti on August 5th, with his great fleet of four thousand men and a treasure chest filled with negotiable currency. On August 25th, Admiral DeBarras' fleet, conveying Rochambeau's siege artillery, sailed from Newport, Rhode Island to the Chesapeake. The naval strategy was to overcome the British stronghold at the Chesapeake but DeBarras had to get past the English fleet harbored in New York. God's ways are not our ways. Unexplained confusion surrounded Cornwallis' British commanders who were entrenched in the New York harbors. A mysterious fog enshrouded the harbor at the Battle of Brooklyn Hill. Perhaps miraculously, the English failed to grasp the significance of French naval strategies unfolding in front of them in New York harbor.

By August 30, 1781, the French were now masters of the Chesapeake. On September 5th, French officers who brought General Washington news of De Grasse's plenary tactics noted that they had never seen a man express so much joy. They wrote:

"The General 'acted like a child whose every wish [prayer] had been gratified.'"[112]

The British fleet departed the Virginia coast. Washington and the allied armies under him, commanded by Rochambeau, Lafayette and Saint-Simon, along with 1,500 of the ever faithful Virginia militia, besieged Cornwallis' stronghold at Yorktown, beginning on September 30. On October 17, 1781, the defeated Cornwallis surrendered.[113]

Thirteen United States Colonies sent Commissioners to Paris to negotiate peace with Great Britain.

Throughout the long negotiations, Washington remained calm, humble and a voice of peace in the United States. A definitive treaty was finally concluded on September 3, 1783.

CHAPTER EIGHT

America's Prosperity

"...I hope someday or another, we shall become a
storehouse and granary for the world."[114]
—*George Washington*

*H*istory has canonized George Washington as the most esteemed of the Founding Fathers for many reasons. Without his transfiguring faith, personal self-sacrifice, expertise and, most significantly of all, victory on the battlefield, the Declaration of Independence would have been a seal of defeat and certain death for the signers. Washington's amazingly modest, brilliant and severely tested leadership assured that the extraordinary "government of the people, by the people and for the people" did not crumble in the sands of humanity's unrealized dreams.

Washington, a big boned powerful man with high cheeks, piercing blue eyes, insightful intelligence, steady humor and consistent patience willingly carried America's dreams for freedom on his brave shoulders. He did not work alone. No one does. He surrounded himself with outstanding leaders of every region, faith and national background. However, he made it clear that he would always bow before Divine Providence, from Whom all blessings, including prosperity flow, and those who would serve with him would necessarily do the same.

Without personal freedom, there is no prosperity. Washington's practical, down to earth faith lives in the spiritual philosophy of the American system of private enterprise that first appeared before the world in the Declaration of Independence. From his childhood, Washington had an indomitable belief that every person is gifted and intended by God to live in peace, prosperity and the pursuit of happiness. Washington kept a daily journal in which he faithfully recorded where and how his time and money were spent. His records show that he was frugal by nature. However, he expended lavishly to enrich his family, his home, his slaves—whom he treated as citizens of Mount Vernon at a time when Virginia accorded them no rights at all—his

Country and countrymen. Washington was aware that prayer, hard work, sacrificial discipline, and God's reciprocal gift of wisdom are constant companions of those who succeed in life.

Washington's colleagues in the pursuit of American private enterprise were a formidable team. Benjamin Franklin of Pennsylvania, John Adams of Massachusetts, Roger Sherman of Connecticut, Robert R. Livingston of New York and Thomas Jefferson of Virginia, men of deep spiritual and political conviction, drafted the Declaration of Independence in 1776. They submitted it to the Continental Congress on the twenty-eighth of June in that year. On July 4th, 1776, after vigorous debate, men representing the thirteen united colonies on the North American continent ratified the document, thereby declaring themselves and their constituents a free, independent nation in the world. By one signature, that of John Hancock, President of the Congress, the Declaration of Independence became a beacon of freedom to the entire world, and created a land of unparalleled prosperity. On August 2, 1776, fifty-five of the fifty-six signers also placed their signatures on the Declaration of Independence. Finally and before year-end, Matthew Thornton's signature completed the unanimous document that gave life to the United States of America.

The spirit of individual and financial freedom became a gale force in the colonies. A careful review of the language of the Declaration unveils the contempt the founders held for unjust policies and corrupt authority. Americans were unwilling to accept anyone's alleged divine right to kill, exploit, pillage and loot private property. That courageous position, though brave, was as dangerous and costly then as it remains today.

With the passage of more than two hundred years, and thousands of miles of ocean to separate them from European shores, the colonists had survived by growing in wisdom and renewed reverence for the laws and rewards of God. The Bible, readily available in the colonies, breathed the power of God's grace into the hearts of God-fearing men and women. Their heightened awareness of the spirit of liberty under just law forbade them from bowing before tyranny from any source. The Sacred Word enjoined them to protect themselves from human predators, even at the cost of their own lives. Therefore, the Declaration of Independence was written with the ink of revolution that would soon turn to blood. Only faith in God's powerful Providence could spur such patriotism.

Washington and his colleagues perceived a natural aristocracy among men, grounded in virtue and talents.[115] The idolatrous ancient aristocracy with its unearned privileges and wealth was not for America. George Washington and his colleagues lived their belief that the Creator breathes all people out of His Heart of love. Each comes into the world endowed with certain unalienable rights, among which are life, liberty and the pursuit of happiness. Embracing scriptural principles as a blueprint for human development, the Founders inspired people of the thirteen Colonies to rise to the heights of fortitude and courage. Americans sought to earn the Biblical rewards of prosperity, long life, health, wisdom, peace steeped in the way, the truth and the light of God's laws and promises.

The American Founders, under Washington's leadership, drew deeply upon Christian roots and Christian concepts of duty among Colonists of every belief, race and nation. The seriousness of this commitment pervades the language of the Declaration of Independence and the Constitution with its Bill of Rights which followed in 1791. The Bible illumined the way to liberty and its rewards, prosperity and happiness in the new republic, one nation under God. All citizens were expected to ascend the heights of spiritual righteousness.

In the war against England, Washington and his coterie pledged their lives, their fortunes and their sacred honor as surety for the success of their cause.[116] Such sacrifice is the heart of the ancient Christian ethic centered in the cross of Jesus Christ.

The signers of the Declaration of Independence included themselves in the first group called to shed their blood if necessary. Their stated goal was to bring forth a new nation conceived in liberty and dedicated to the proposition that all people are in fact divinely created equal before God. As such each is entitled to life, liberty and the pursuit of happiness. With the stroke of their pen on that document, each man became a notorious traitor, and punishable by death under English law.

Recognizing that a brutal war lay on the horizon, for tyrants hold fast to their prey, General Washington rallied the colonists who were for the most part farmers, fur traders, merchants and fishermen. His singular leadership passionately prepared these peace loving men to shed their last drop of blood rather than yield their property, their livelihood and their freedom. Tyranny and oppression from absentee rulers were incompatible with the winds of liberty that the colonists enjoyed. From the beginning, the underlying principles of the United States included the sacredness and inherent

dignity of each unique human life and the inviolate
right to own and enjoy private property.

By the time Washington was appointed Commander
in chief of the Revolutionary Forces, he was married to
Martha Dandridge Custis, a wealthy widow with two
small children. She was one of the richest women in
Virginia.[117] Their life together at Mount Vernon was full
and quite pleasing to the General. Mrs. Washington,
though plump, was small in stature, five feet tall. She
was not born to wealth but inherited it from her first
husband. Those who knew her said she was modest and
sweet tempered, not at all spoiled by her great wealth,
which passed into George Washington's hands at their
marriage. She was "…a lady in manners and in conduct
about whom there was never a word of scandal."[118]

Her biographer, Joseph E. Fields writes of Martha
Washington:

"In many ways, Martha Washington was the
ideal woman for the new American republic.
She was not born of the aristocracy, but she
gained the admiration and respect of all classes
of people. She was devoted to family and home,
but she readily made personal sacrifices to join
her husband in his public duties…During the

Presidency, she was called both dignified and democratic as she forged the role of the President's wife that would be followed for generations to come. She neither sought nor relished her public positions, but carried out the duties that were thrust upon her with enormous consideration and care. Her simple appearance bespoke quality rather than ostentation..."[119]

Abigail Adams, wife of John Adams wrote:

"Mrs. Washington is one of those unassuming characters which create Love and esteem." In her presence, Mrs. Adams admitted she found herself "much more deeply impressed than I ever did before their Majesties of Britain."[120]

The Commander in Chief loved his wife dearly. Martha's virtues certainly influenced Washington. Her calming presence and steadfastness in his life provided comfort, support and the joy of her two young children whom Washington raised as his own. Mrs. Washington, though she never bore a child for the General, was with him at Valley Forge, Boston, and other places of difficulty during the Revolutionary War. She cared for his beloved Mount Vernon during his long absences and entertained dignitaries, statesmen and ordinary citizens for him during his long career in government. She carried out his wishes concerning the slaves of Mount Vernon, educating the children and emancipating them all.

Martha and George Washington's kindness and commitment to one another exemplified the ideals of the times in the United States where godliness implies an individual God-given right to think, believe and respond to God's divine presence without coercion. They cherished their rights to own and protect private property without undue disturbance and to pursue personal happiness. George Washington as Founding Father claimed for himself, his loved ones and those he served individual, personal freedom of thought, religious belief, political persuasion, and a life grounded in the laws of God and of nature.

In a public address at a great civic banquet in Philadelphia, on April 20, 1789, celebrating his unanimous election as First President of the United States, Washington said:

"When I contemplate the interposition of Providence, as it was manifested in guiding us through the Revolution, in preparing us for the reception of a general government, and in conciliating the good will of the people of America towards one another after its adoption, I feel myself oppressed and almost overwhelmed with a sense of divine munificence. I feel that nothing is due to my personal agency in all these complicated and wonderful events, except what can simply be attributed to the exertions of an honest zeal for the good of my country.

" If I have distressing apprehensions, that I shall not be able to justify the too exalted expectations of my countrymen, I am supported under the pressure of such uneasy reflections by a confidence that the most gracious Being, who has hitherto watched over the interests and averted the perils of the United States, will never suffer so fair an inheritance to become a prey to anarchy, despotism, or any other species of oppression."[121]

To understand God as the source of American prosperity, one need only consider the number and variety of active, thriving churches, temples, synagogues, mosques, sports arenas, schools, universities and businesses per capita in the United States. The faith of our Founder lives in the accomplishments of our youth, in the output of our industry, in technological, diplomatic, military, social and medical advances that break global curses of isolation, ignorance, poverty, sickness and war.

American prosperity is rooted in the glorious diversity and spiritual depth of its varied people. In no small measure, the presence and cultural heritage of Native Americans added dignity and grace to the emerging United States. Indians, as Columbus mistakenly named them, welcomed Europeans as "men from heaven."[122] They taught the newcomers how to farm, fish, hunt and survive in North America. Medicine men, citing the ways of the "Great Spirit", provided drug remedies that were sought after by the more enlightened because of their heightened effectiveness against disease. Whether knowingly or through Divine Providence, early Americans embraced Godly virtues as they created an enduring governmental framework in which individual expression of love, commitment, labor and thrift are rewarded with prosperity.

Reflecting his own vision of prosperous steward-ship, Washington was an honest and shrewd business-man.[123] His business education was rooted in the Bible. In the book of Genesis, the Bible recounts God's plan for managing financial resources. Beginning with revelations to Abraham, Christianity's father in faith, God

"*Gaze not at the marks or blemishes of others, and ask not how they came. What you may speak in secret to your friend, deliver not before others.*"

8   *"Then their faith-filled Commander in Chief, in full view of his troops, knelt in the snow to implore the blessings and providence of Almighty God on the dedicated men who carried the hopes and dreams of freedom in their hearts."*

offers rewards and punishments that affect human wealth, health and happiness.

When Abraham was seventy-five years old, he heard the voice of the Lord commanding him: "Go forth from the land of your kinfolk and from your father's house to the land that I will show you."[124] This was a difficult order, yet one that God would issue time and again throughout ensuing centuries to countless others. God told Abraham to leave everyone and everything he knew and loved except for his half sister Sarah, daughter of his father but not of his mother, whom he had taken as his wife. She was quite beautiful. Things went well for Abraham wherever he wandered.

The Nomadic Abraham arrived in Egypt without money and perhaps afraid. Because Sarah was so enticing, the Pharaoh took her for his wife, believing that she was merely Abraham's sister. But God does not tolerate adultery for long. Pharaoh's house was struck with severe plagues. When the afflicted Pharaoh realized the source of his suffering, he commanded that Abraham take back Sarah, along with restitution of herds and flocks, male and female slaves, asses and camels. Only then did the plagues abate in the Pharaoh's personal household and throughout his kingdom.

Abraham and Sarah were now rich in livestock, silver and gold. They were financially rewarded for Abraham's obedience to the voice of God which sent him and Sarah forth into distant, unfamiliar, mysterious places with nothing but faith in God's providence as their guiding light. Abraham and Sarah continued their travels in obedience to the Lord's voice which guided Abraham.

Now steward of vast resources and assets, Abraham not only had responsibility for Sarah, but he also was called to actively manage diverse people, flocks and herds of animals. Abraham, investing multiple currencies became in effect an international banker and diplomat, negotiating, trading and engaging in gorilla wars along the way. Hearing the Lord, he became expert at leveraging and bartering his passage across the desert in obedience to the calls of the Lord.

George Washington would have been a student of Abraham's relationship with God. He, like Abraham[125] invoked the Lord by name in prayer. The more adroit Abraham became at listening to the Lord, discerning God's will and obeying, the more successful he became in his accomplishments. So also it was with George Washington. Abraham learned that no encounter on the earth is a coincidence. Opportunity for improvement of people, places and things lies hidden in every meeting. Washington too, a faithful son of Abraham, lived by that truth.

Guided by their Christian faith, Washington and his wife were quite compatible and he was faithful to her.[126] Washington never engaged in duels though he was an able swordsman with developed fencing skills, nor resorted to violence with his peers or underlings. He was slow to anger, but fierce in battle when aroused.[127] Washington preferred the presence of polite ladies and gentlemen at Mount Vernon rather than rough, unpolished soldiers and frontiersmen.[128] He was distinguished for his courtesy. Biographer John R. Alden reported of Washington:

> "He developed a cool and discriminating judgment and with it a remarkable ability to take advantage of the insights of other men."[129]

Washington, with his gentle Martha at his side, enjoyed many of life's pleasures. He drank fine tea, sipped excellent wine, danced at social events, played cards and billiards with gentlemen and shared his pleasing sense of humor. Though Washington encouraged learning, he never did so at the expense of duty to entrusted assets and obligations. He believed that education without faith was a waste. He bought his stepson books of theology, philosophy, arithmetic, science, history, English poetry and travel. He consistently encouraged his stepson to grow in consonance with his station in life as a Christian and a patriot. He also urged him to learn enlightened ways of farming the fertile Virginia land. Washington at heart believed as a farmer that he was a trustee of God's earth. A true environmentalist, he loved the earth's munificence. His great love for nature inspired him to become one of the most successful land speculators of his times.[130]

George and Martha Washington were generous stewards of God's goodness to them. Their joy was to share their blessings. One biographer Lonnelle Aikman writes of a typical Christmas dinner at Mount Vernon:

"Christmas dinner with the Washington's at Mount Vernon brings on the usual good food and good conversation. Many guests who sat at this table wrote glowingly of both. One recalled an impressive menu of 'roasted pig, boiled leg of lamb, roasted fowls, beef, peas, lettuce, cucumbers, artichokes, etc., puddings, tarts, etc., etc.' For drinks there was a choice of wines, beer, or cider. It was then the custom to serve dinner in mid-afternoon, tea at six, and supper, if desired, at about nine."[131]

Washington was a temperate man who led by example. He forbade vulgarity, womanizing and profanity among his troops, employees and slaves. He expressed his views on the dangers of consuming intoxicating liquor to one of his overseers.

> "...[R]efrain from spirituous liquors; they will prove your ruin if you do not. Consider how little a drunken man differs from a beast; the latter is not endowed with reason, the former deprives himself of it; and when that is the case, acts like a brute, annoying and disturbing everyone around him. Nor is this all, nor as it respects himself, the worst of it. By degrees, it renders a person feeble, and not only unable to serve others but to help himself; and being an act of his own, he falls from a state of usefulness into contempt, and at length suffers, if not perishes in penury and want."[132]

George Washington, generous with his time, talents and assets, accordingly was rewarded by God. He served on the vestry of his Episcopal Church and was a Justice of the Peace for the Commonwealth of Virginia, Fairfax County. During his lifetime, God generously endowed him with the gift of wisdom, by which Washington increased rather than dissipated his wealth. Though he had only a life interest in Mount Vernon, he was able to acquire seven thousand acres adjacent to his Potomac River front property. Two hundred years later, much of the world seeks the ways of freedom and prosperity that Washington found in his lifetime.

CHAPTER NINE

Washington's Legacy

"Integrity and firmness is all I can promise; these, be
the voyage long or short, never shall forsake me
although I may be deserted by all men."[133]
—George Washington

*W*ashington's influence was extensive. Though
he remained active, the General resigned his
commission at Annapolis in 1783 and retired to his
beloved Mount Vernon. His advice however was widely sought in the formation of the new national and state
governments. Washington, who wrote at least 4,000
letters in his lifetime duly noted his recollection of the
business of his life of service years later in 1797:

"...[U]nless someone pops in unexpectedly, Mrs. Washington and I will do what has not been (done) by us in nearly 20 years – that is sit down to dinner by ourselves."[134]

The spirituality of the times which Washington so faithfully embraced and exemplified is discernible in the humanitarian nature of the disciplines undertaken in the newly developing United States. There was widespread conviction that the gentleman of pleasure was a plague to himself as well as to his society, and particularly in times of crisis.[135] Consequently, inventions proliferated and nature's secrets were investigated assiduously. Literature and the arts flourished. Business and commerce thrived. It was understood that the vices and foibles of society derive fundamentally from a lack of work discipline and the virtuous habits which the maintaining of good fortune require.[136]

Godly men of destiny met in the State House at Philadelphia beginning in May of 1787 to draft a Federal Constitution for the United States. Washington once again left his home at Mount Vernon to serve his country as a representative from Virginia. Under his watchful, though mostly silent leadership, the Federal Convention created a framework for the

United States government that endures to this day. Dickinson, a Pennsylvanian, announced a clear break with the intellectuals of the "Age of Reason" thereby setting the tone for the document with the words: "Experience must be our only guide. Reason may mislead us."

Embracing the freedom of their newly ratified Constitution, the people of the United States elected their first President, a hero whose tested leadership was totally steeped in commitment to God's ways. Washington was their unanimous choice. His new job was Herculean. Documents, dreams and realities of the newborn United States of America sprang to life in the nurturing light of George Washington's faith filled Christian spirituality.

Moderns rarely understand the depth of Washington's religious conviction that "...God would hold him accountable for the ultimate meaning of American independence as revealed by history."[137] Disobedience to God's ways, as they knew them, continued to be the cardinal transgression of the times and especially under Washington's watch. Racial heterogeneity and social structure ranged from sophisticated, rich East Coast merchants to rebellious frontiersmen.

Such diversity was obviously God's plan for the new nation from the beginning.

George Washington was so beloved by the populace that he could have allowed himself to become King of America. Many in fact desired to crown him. Such adulation was not attractive to the first President of the United States. After having served two full terms in office, in retirement he chose to remain an ordinary citizen and return to his family duties at Mount Vernon. Power did not corrupt this leader for he was a highly tested bearer of wisdom and humility.

The final years of Washington's life passed peacefully and productively at his beloved Mount Vernon along the shores of the Potomac River. An analysis of his home life, management of his plantation and writings disclose hints of Washington's deep spiritual detachment from all that is not of God, for God, with God, and in God. George Washington acquired that spiritual freedom during a lifetime of service to his family, community and nation that required him to ascend the mountains of asceticism.

By 1799, Washington spoke frequently and in quite a matter of fact manner of the limited days that remained to him on earth. He was keenly aware that he was approaching the "Biblical three score and ten."

"He worked strenuously to organize his affairs, all for which he was responsible in such a manner so as to bring no burden upon anyone…'that no reproach may attach itself to me when I have taken my departure for the land of spirits.'"[138]

After his youngest brother died in the summer of 1799, Washington lamented: "I am the first, and am now the last of my father's children by the second marriage who remain. When I shall be called upon to follow them is known only to the Giver of life."[139]

Martha Washington was aware of her spouse's premonition of impending death. She wrote the following letter to a relative on September 18, 1799.

"At midsummer the General had a dream so deeply impressed on his mind that he could not shake it off for several days. He dreamed that he and I were sitting in the summer-house, conversing about the happy life we had spent, and looking forward to many more years on the earth, when suddenly there was a great light all around us, and then an almost invisible figure of a sweet angel stood by my side and whispered in my ear. I suddenly turned pale and then began to vanish from his sight and he was left alone. I had just risen from the bed when he awoke and told me his dream, saying, 'You know a contrary result indicated by dreams may be expected. I may soon leave you.' I tried to drive from his mind the sadness that had taken possession of it, by laughing at the absurdity of being disturbed by an idle dream, which, at the worst, indicated that I would not be taken from him; but I could not, and it was not until after dinner that he recovered any cheerfulness. I found in the library, a few days afterwards, some scraps of paper which showed that he had been making a Will, and had copied it…"[140]

Historical records reveal Washington on December 9, five days before his death. His nephew recounted:

"It was a bright frosty morning; he had taken his usual ride and the clear health flush on his cheek and his sprightly manner, brought the remark from both of us that we had never seen the General look so well. I have sometimes thought him decidedly the handsomest man I ever saw; and when in a lively mood, so full of pleasantry, so agreeable to all with whom he associated, that I could hardly realize that he was the same Washington whose dignity awed all who approached him."[141]

On December 12, the master of Mount Vernon mounted his horse by ten o'clock. His thoughts are unknown. His ride included his entire estate at Mount Vernon. He certainly saw the homes of three hundred slaves. Washington doggedly, at great personal sacrifice, and contrary to the culture and mores of his time, refused to sell or disperse slave families. Washington, fatherly as he was, forbade separation of slave families. His slaves, legally his personal property, were intermarried with Martha's slaves over whom he had no direct authority. Washington, graced as he was, disallowed total disruption of the family life of the slaves of Mount Vernon should he emancipate only his own, thereby sending them far away. At that time, slaves had no protection of the laws in Virginia. Their entire well-being depended on their owner's decisions. Washington respected his slaves as children of God. At Mount Vernon, he provided the equivalent of village life for them fairly, yet generously, both in difficult and comfortable economic times.

General Washington wrote of his dilemma concerning his slaves to his nephew Robert Lewis.

"To sell the overplus [unneeded slaves] I cannot because I am prejudiced against this kind of traffic in the human species; to hire them out is almost as bad, because they cannot be disposed of in families to any advantage, and to divide families I have an aversion."[142]

Washington was a visionary who during his lifetime understood that slavery of any kind is unjust and immoral.[143] By his final Will and Testament, he decreed that all Mount Vernon slaves be freed upon the death of his wife. By his providential reversionary interest in Mount Vernon, he retained legal rights to accomplish that emancipation. Washington directed his Executors to provide for the aged blacks out of the assets of his estate. Washington further provided that, before slave children be emancipated, they be taught to read and write and brought to some useful occupation, even though the laws of Virginia forbade the education of slaves.[144] Martha carried out her husband's wishes. Within a year of his death, slave children who had been taught to read and write were among the plantation's three hundred emancipated slaves.

Washington was a tested man who appreciated the power, beauty, bounty and cruelty of nature. Perhaps he saw in the wonders of nature a tiny hint of God's presence. Washington, with his much loved staff worked tirelessly to beautify Mount Vernon, to make it bountiful and prosperous for all. Here was a man called to heal and restore creation, not just for himself, and the few who surrounded him, but for all of us too.

Washington had deep gifts of the spirit. With him, these gifts were safe and available for the good of humanity because he allowed himself to be guided by the very wisdom of God Almighty. Nothing displays his kinship with God more profoundly than the circumstances of his death.

Washington's deathbed suffering was accepted lovingly by America's Founding Father as a gentle gift of God's will. He realized that anything short of perfect abandonment to Providence would be the ultimate defilement of his immortal soul and consummate defeat. By this time in his life, Washington had fought the good fight. Any deep-seated behavior reflecting insensitivity to sin was mollified by the time the Founding Father succumbed to death's call. Washington's faithful secretary and executive assistant,

Tobias Lear recorded some of the circumstances surrounding his last hours.[145]

Washington's final and greatest battle began in the rain that dreary December day in 1799. Washington rode on despite the inclement weather for he had work to do on his plantation. Faith must have works to express itself, personally and in the service of others.[146] Many depended on Washington for their daily bread. He chose to bring to perfection his earthly activities ("works"). Washington the planter knew the rains water God's earth with new life. Driving rain did not deter the master from his daily duties.

A change in the weather brought first snow and then sleet that day. During Washington's five-hour ride around the plantation, the sleet changed into cold, steady rain that turned again to snow. When he came into the house, his face was ruddy, the back of his neck covered with snow. But he said he felt quite well. Washington ate his meal that evening and those who were with him found him to be as hearty and thoughtful as usual.

The next day, on December 13, the plantation was covered with snow. Washington, experiencing a sore throat, stayed in doors for most of the day. When the snow stopped at four o'clock, he went outside to the front lawn to mark specific trees to be removed. That evening, after their evening meal, George and Martha sat by the fire in the parlor. Though his voice was hoarse, Washington read aloud from gazettes for her edification. When it was suggested that he take something for his cold, Washington said he never took anything for a cold. Rather, he preferred to "let it go as it came."[147]

During the night, in the early hours of December 14, Washington experienced severe chills and fever. His great difficulty in breathing awakened his wife sometime between two and three A.M. She saw that he was in much distress and could hardly speak. Though Martha desired to summon a servant, Washington restrained her fearing for her health in the cold room. He endured his difficulties silently, lovingly encouraging Martha to go back to sleep. Finally a morning servant arrived to lay the fire at seven A.M. Martha then quickly summoned help for the ailing General.

By now he could not swallow, and his words were becoming somewhat unintelligible. During the next thirteen hours, he was bled four times. Of course, the procedure served only to weaken him further. Washington mentioned about his throat: "Tis very sore." Other than that, no complaints were heard at all. He by now had a severe streptococcus infection.[148]

Washington insisted upon getting dressed that day. After sitting by the fire in his room for about two hours without relief, he returned to his bed. By four thirty, Washington quietly said to the doctors in attendance:

> "I feel myself going. I thank you for your atten-
> tion. You had better not take any more trouble
> about me; but let me go off quietly; I cannot
> last long."[149]

He asked for Martha to join him. His courage allowed her and others gathered around him to see that suffering is a gift and a test of a soul's capacity to love.[150]

He who had escaped death so many times on the battlefield knew well there is a time to die. No one disputes the brilliant faith of George Washington. Though as far as is known, there is currently nothing available contemporaneously written about the following story, it is widely circulated that Washington, or perhaps those around him sent for his Minister to join him in his preparations to meet his Maker. In the mysterious ways of Divine Providence, the Minister was nowhere to be found on such short notice. The only clergyman available, so the legend that circulates to this day holds, was

Reverend Neale, a priest from the Maryland Province of the Society of Jesus. George Washington, forever the man of destiny, is said to have accepted his fate peacefully. The immortal Founding Father of the United States, great grandson of a persecuted Anglican Catholic priest, so some say, humbly confessed his sins, received the Blessed Sacrament, and final anointing with Holy Oil.[151]

During the last hours of Washington's life, three medical providers were in attendance. His lifelong friend, Dr. Craik, Dr. Elisha Cullen Dick of Alexandria and Dr. Gustavus Richard Brown of Port Tobacco conferred about the ailing General's condition:

> "Drs. Craik and Brown agreed on the diagnosis of quinsy (an extreme form of tonsillitis) and urged further debilitating treatment—more bleeding and blisters and also purges. Dr. Dick, who at thirty-seven was by far the youngest of the three, argued that Washington was suffering from a 'violent inflammation of the membranes of the throat, which it had almost closed, and which if not immediately arrested, would result in death.' He urged an operation that would open the trachea below the infection so

Washington could breathe...Down the years doctors have speculated on the nature of Washington's illness. One guess is diphtheria, another a virulent streptococcus infection of the throat. Either disease would, in the state of medicine at that time, have been fatal regardless of the treatment prescribed."[152]

By ten o'clock that night, Washington spoke to his secretary Lear:

"I am just going. Have me decently buried, and do not let my body be put into a vault in less than two days after I am dead."

Washington looked directly at Lear:
"Do you understand me?" he commanded.

Lear responded: "Yes, Sir."
"'Tis well." said Washington.

Martha sat by the foot of the bed. Lear held the General's hand. Servants, doctors and others stood near the door. Washington's breathing became easier as the hour passed ten. He lay quietly. Gently Washington withdrew his hand to feel his own pulse. Suddenly, a change in the General's countenance occurred and his fingers slipped away from his wrist. Two elements, body and soul had been mysteriously united in one reality for 67 years; in the blink of an eye, the humanity of George Washington separated from his immortal soul. The General had surrendered his last command.

Martha calmly asked: "Is he gone?" Lear, choking with emotion nodded affirmatively. "Tis well." she said, echoing the General's last words. "All is over now. I have no more trials to pass through. I shall soon follow him."[153] It has been said:

> "Martha's fortitude reflected that of the General. The quietness with which he had borne his pain through the long day and she her sorrow made them the more poignant for those who merely watched and worked."[154]

George Washington was buried in the family vault at Mount Vernon on the 18th of December in 1799. A solemn procession to the vault was led by cavalry, infantrymen and the guard, all with arms reversed, followed by the band, the clergy, and the General's horse. Four lieutenants of the Virginia militia carried the bier. Six honorary pall bearers marched, three on each side. Family, friends and dignitaries followed. Those who lived and worked on the Washington estates comprised the rest of the procession. The Minister, Reverend Davis read the Order of Burial from the Episcopal Prayer Book. Washington's rector gave a brief eulogy. When all was finished, minute guns from Robert Hamilton's schooner, anchored close by in the Potomac, fired their final salute to America's Founding Father. Eleven artillery cannon answered.

King William IV, son of George III of England unabashedly declared George Washington the greatest man who ever lived. Congressman Light Horse Harry Lee of Virginia entered into the Congressional Record that Washington was "first in war, first in peace and first in the hearts of his countrymen."

Washington, true son of the Republic in deed and spirit, looked and learned, served, loved and died that America might always be one nation under God with liberty and justice for all. God was with George Washington. He chose him as Founding Father of the United States. Washington was faithful to the end.

America need never fear. Indomitable faith, trust in God's merciful love, obedience to the word of God, sacrificial service, gracious stewardship are George Washington's most enduring legacy. God's grace is sufficient for all times.

Afterword

Excerpts From George Washington's Farewell Address

United States, 19th September, 1796

Friends, & Fellow—Citizens.

...I will only say, that I have, with good intentions, contributed towards the Organization and Administration of the government, the best exertions of which a very fallible judgment was capable....

...my feelings do not permit me to suspend the deep acknowledgment of that debt of gratitude which I owe to my beloved country, for the many honors it has conferred upon me; still more for the steadfast confidence with which it has supported me; and for the opportunities I have thence enjoyed of manifesting my inviolable attachment, by services faithful and persevering, though in usefulness unequal to my zeal. If benefits have resulted to our country from these services, let it always be remembered to your praise, and as an instructive example in our annals, that, under circumstances in which the Passions agitated in every direction were liable to mislead, amidst appearances sometimes dubious, vicissitudes of fortune often discouraging, in situations in which not infrequently want of Success has countenanced the spirit of criticism, the constancy of your support was the essential prop of the efforts, and a guarantee of the plans by which they were effected. Profoundly penetrated with this idea, I shall carry it with me to my grave, as a strong incitement to unceasing vows that Heaven may continue to you the choicest tokens of its beneficence—that your Union & brotherly affection may be perpetual—that the free constitution, which is the work of your hands, may be sacredly maintained—that its Administration in every department may be stamped with wisdom and Virtue—that, in fine, the happiness of the people of these States, under the auspices of liberty, may be made complete, by so careful a preservation and so prudent a use of this blessing as will acquire to them the glory of recommending it to the applause, the affection—and adoption of every nation which is yet a stranger to it.

The Unity of Government which constitutes you one people is also now dear to you. It is justly so; for it is a main Pillar in the Edifice of your real independence, the support of your tranquillity at home; your peace abroad; of your safety; of your prosperity; of that very Liberty which you so highly prize. But as it is easy to foresee, that from different causes & from different quarters, much pains will be taken, many artifices employed, to weaken in your minds the conviction of this truth; as this is the point in your political fortress against which the batteries of internal & external enemies will be most constantly and actively (though often covertly & insidiously) directed, it is of infinite moment, that you should properly estimate the immense value of your national Union to your collective & individual happiness; that you should cherish a cordial, habitual & immovable attachment to it; accustoming yourselves to think and speak of it as of the Palladium of your political safety and prosperity; watching for its preservation with jealous anxiety; discountenancing whatever may suggest even a suspicion that it can in any event be abandoned, and indignantly frowning upon the first dawning of every attempt to alienate any portion of our Country from the rest, or to enfeeble the sacred ties which now link together the various parts.

For this you have every inducement of sympathy and interest. Citizens by birth or choice, of a common country, that country has a right to concentrate your affections. The name of American, which belongs to you, in your national capacity, must always exalt the just pride of Patriotism, more than any appellation derived from local discriminations. With slight shades of difference, you have the same Religion, Manners, Habits & political Principles. You have in a common cause fought & triumphed together. The independence & liberty you possess are the work of joint councils, and joint efforts—of common dangers, sufferings and successes.

But these considerations, however powerfully they address themselves to your sensibility are greatly outweighed by those which apply more immediately to your Interest. Here every portion of our country finds the most commanding motives for carefully guarding & preserving the Union of the whole.

...[Y]our union ought to be considered as a main prop of your liberty, and that the love of the one ought to endear to you the preservation of the other.

...With such powerful and obvious motives to Union, affecting all parts of our country, while experience shall not have demonstrated its impracticability, there will always be reason, to distrust the patriotism of those, who in any quarter may endeavor to weaken its bands.

…Of all the dispositions and habits which lead to political prosperity, Religion and morality are indispensable supports. In vain would that man claim the tribute of Patriotism, who should labor to subvert these great Pillars of human happiness, these firmest props of the duties of Men & citizens. The mere Politician, equally with the pious man ought to respect & to cherish them. …. Whatever may be conceded to the influence of refined education on minds of peculiar structure—reason & experience both forbid us to expect that National morality can prevail in exclusion of religious principle.

…Observe good faith & justice towards all Nations. Cultivate peace & Religion & morality enjoin this conduct; and can it be that good policy does not equally enjoin it? It will be worthy of a free, enlightened, and, at no distant period, a great Nation, to give to mankind the magnanimous and too novel example of a People always guided by an exalted justice and benevolence.[155]

Finally

George Washington believed that people receive the power to live happy, prosperous and healthy lives from Almighty God. Such divine gifts, he warned, are reciprocal. He articulated duties of all people in his Thanksgiving Proclamation, October 3, 1789.

"...[I]t is the duty of all Nations to acknowledge the Providence of Almighty God, to obey His will, to be grateful for His benefits, and humbly to implore His protection and favor."[156]

Acknowledgments

Caring friends have played a special role in bringing this book to life. John Donovan's long-suffering inspiration kept me at work on this book over the years. Thank you, John. I would especially like to thank Professor Thomas King, S.J., and Professor Paul Chaufey, S. J., Georgetown University, and Professor Robert Faricy, S.J., Gregorian University, for their help and guidance with this book.

Throughout the research on this book, many people who love their country helped me. I am deeply grateful. Rosemary and Carroll Carter, descendant of Daniel Carroll, Signer of the Declaration of Independence inspired me to continue. Michael Novak, who provided the intellectual analysis that brings credence to the spiritual journey of George Washington reflected in these pages, deserves much gratitude. Heartfelt thanks to Theresa Martin, Martha and Bernie McWatters, Ambassador Margaret M Heckler, Msgr. Thomas Duffy, Rev. John Guest, Rev. Ruth Schofield, Rev. Adrian Van Kaam, Rev. John

Sanford, Rev. Victor Potopov, Susan Muto, David
Manuel, Lillian Miao, Harold Cassidy, Bob Weil, Joelle
Delbourgo, Robert Sensale, Mary Rourke, Mary Noel
and Bill Page, Walter and Cornelia Covington
Smithwick, descendant of Rev. John Gano, Baptist
preacher who was George Washington's personal chap-
lain during the Revolutionary War, Betty Skinner,
Virginia and Frank Pelly, Bill Hammond, Reus and
Estella Ruiz, Ishbel and John McGregor, Betty and
Nicholas Bova, Sherrill and Bob Baker, Pat and Joe
Barba, Rocky and Barbara Martino, Tom Espinoza.
Your kindness, hospitality and encouragement made
this book possible.

Bob Angelotti has been instrumental in all aspects
of this book. Thank you, Bob.

The Mount Vernon Ladies' Association, The
National Park Service, and especially the Valley Forge
Museum provided invaluable insights into the spirit of
George Washington reflected in this book. I can never
thank each of you who work in hallowed places
enough. These citizens have labored with heroic valor
to preserve the facts of Washington's life for future generations and are deserving of great gratitude.

My appreciation is deep and lasting for George Washington's biographers and is matched only by my admiration.

Thank you Michael Denneny for your editorial expertise. Frederic Flach, M.D., K.C.H.S., and Kevin Moran deserve heartfelt thanks.

This book, a labor of love, is not the work of an academic or historian. Rather, it takes its place in a pattern of life dictated by demands of family, professional responsibility and community commitments. My husband Ed's patience, wit and wisdom are reflected in this small book. I am so very grateful. Our children and grandchildren, Betsy and Derek Minno, Mary Christian and Ricky, Ted and Jennifer Connell, Lilly and Teddy, William and Regina Connell and their infant are my great teachers. I thank God for them and pray they, and all future generations, will always have the privilege of living the American dream.

Notes

[1] Letter to Richard Henderson, June 19, 1788, George
Washington, Writings Volume 29 p.520, as quoted in
*Maxims of George Washington, Political, Social, Moral,
and Religious*, Collected and Arranged by John
Frederick Schroeder (Mount Vernon, VA: Mount
Vernon Ladies Association, 1989), 51.

[2] Janice T. Connell, *Meetings with Mary* (New York:
Ballantine Books, 1995), 139.

[3] Matthew. 7: 7,8

[4] See Chapter 2.

[5] See Chapter 7.

[6] John R. Alden, *George Washington, A Biography* (Baton
Rouge, LA: Louisiana State University Press, 1884), 25.

[7] Ibid., 26.

[8] Ibid., 29.

[9] Letter to Governor Dinwiddie, April 7, 1756, George
Washington, Writings Volume 1, p. 300, as quoted in
Maxims of George Washington, 110.

[10] George Washington, Writings Volume 1, p. 325, as quoted in *Maxims of George Washington*, 123.

[11] Ibid., 16. From Writings Vol. 4 p. 483.

[12] Washington's letter to Bartholomew Dandridge, Philadelphia, March 8, 1797, as quoted in Stephen E. Lucas, ed., *The Quotable George Washington* (Madison, WI: Madison House Publishers, Inc. 1999), 50.

[13] Bradford, M.E. *Founding Fathers: Brief Lives of the Framers of the United States Constitution.* 2nd ed. (Lawrence, KS: University Press of Kansas, 1981), 126.

[14] Samuel E. Morison, and Henry Steele Commager. *The Growth of the American Republic.* 2 vols (New York: Oxford University Press, 1958), 51.

[15] Ibid.

[16] Ibid., 33.

[17] Douglas Southall Freeman, *Washington: A Biography.* An Abridgment by Richard Harwell (New York: Touchstone, 1968), 4.

[18] John T. Phillips II, ed. *George Washington's Rules of Civility* (Leesburg, VA: Goose Creek Productions, 2000), 7.

[19] Rev. Marye was born and raised in Rouen, France. He studied for and was ordained to the priesthood in the Jesuit College of Rouen. In 1726, he fled to England and became an Anglican priest.

[20] *The Rules of Civility and Decent Behavior in Company and Conversation,* ca 1744 are available on the World Wide Web.

21 Gary L. Gregg II, and Matthew Spalding, eds. *Patriot Sage: George Washington and the American Political Tradition* (Wilmington, DE: ISI Books, 1999) quoting Richard Brookhiser, 302.

22 Ibid., 303-304.

23 From a letter to Martha Custis, his fiancee by George Washington written from Fort Cumberland, July 20, 1758.

24 William J. Johnson as quoted *George Washington, The Christian* (Arlington, TX: Christian Liberty Press, 1919), 23.

25 Letter to George Steptoe Washington, Philadelphia, December 5, 1790, as quoted in Lucas, *The Quotable George Washington*, 14.

26 Peter H. Henriques, *George Washington America's First President* (National Park Services: Eastern National Publisher, 2002), 5.

27 Freeman, *Washington: A Biography,*18-19.

28 Bradford, *Founding Fathers*, 127.

29 A life interest that would end at the death of his widow should she survive him, or at his death if he had no spouse at the time of his death.

30 Although 29 of the 56 signers of the Declaration of Independence were graduates of Colonial or British Institutes of higher learning, Washington was not.

31 Morison, and Commager, *The Growth of the American Republic*, 113.

[32] George Washington's Diaries, December 15, 1753. As quoted in Lonnnelle Aikman, *Rider with A Destiny: George Washington* (McLean, VA: Link Press Publishers, 1983, 18-20.

[33] Ibid.

[34] George Washington's letter to his brother John A.Washington, July 18, 1755.

[35] Freeman, *Washington: A Biography*, 86.

[36] Washington as quoted in Morrison and Commager, *The Growth of the American Republic*, 123.

[37] Bradford, *Founding Fathers*, 127.

[38] Aikman, *Rider With A Destiny*, 23. See also James T. Flexner, *Washington The Indispensable Man* (Boston: Little, Brown & Company, 1969), 34, 35 and Freeman, *Washington: A Biography*, 134.

[39] Henriques, *George Washington America's First President*, 13.

[40] Ibid.

[41] Johnson, *George Washington, The Christian*, 41-42.

[42] Letter to Thaddeus Kosciuszko, August 31, 1797, George Washington, Writings Volume 36, p. 22, as quoted in Schroeder, *Maxims of Washington*, 177.

[43] Letter of March 15, 1790, George Washington, Writings Volume 31, p. 22, as quoted in Schroeder, *Maxims of Washington*, 179.

[44] New York, May, 1789, as quoted in Lucas, *The Quotable George Washington*, 81.

45 John Ferling, *Setting the World Ablaze: Washington, Adams, Jefferson, and the American Revolution* (New York: Oxford University Press, 2000), 8, quoting Rosemarie Zagarri, ed. David Humjphreys' *Life of General Washington*, with George Washington's "Remarks" (Athens, GA, 1991) xiii, xx, 5-6.

46 Ibid., 9, quoting George Washington Parke Custis, Recollections and Private Memories of Washington. (New York, 1860), 131, footnote 20, p. 312.

47 Ibid., 10.

48 Ibid., xiv.

49 Gregg and Spalding eds., *Patriot Sage*, 186, quoting Marvin Olasky, *The American Leadership Tradition: Moral Vision From Washington To Clinton* (New York: The Free Press, 1999), 17.

50 Bradford. *Founding Fathers*, 129.

51 Bradford quoting Flexner. *Founding Fathers*, 129.

52 Alden, *George Washington*, 103, 112.

53 Flexner, *Washington, The Indispensable Man*, xvi.

54 Quoted in Gregg and Spalding eds., *Patriot Sage*, 186.

55 Bradford, *Founding Fathers*, 133.

56 Johnson, *George Washington, The Christian*, 112.

57 Barbara W. Tuchman, *The First Salute* (New York: Knopf, 1988), 183.

58 George Washington, *Writings Vol. 11*, 291.

59 William J. Bennett, *Our Sacred Honor* (Nashville, Tennessee: Broadman & Holman Publishers, 1997), 378.

60 George Washington's letter to his Captains on the frontier in 1757.

61 Washington's First Inaugural Address, April 30, 1789.

62 Jay Tolson. *U.S. News and World Report* (September 2002), 14.

63 George Washington. The Circular Address to the States. June 8, 1783, as quoted in Schroeder, *Maxims of Washington*, 21.

64 Ferling, *Setting the World Ablaze*, 267-268.

65 Jacob Needleman. *The American Soul* (New York: Tarcher/ Putnam, 2002), 109.

66 Ibid., 106.

67 Ibid., 107.

68 Washington's Address to the Continental Army before the Battle of Long Island, August 27, 1776, as quoted in Johnson, *George Washington, The Christian*, 82.

69 Alden, *George Washington*, 12.

70 Johnson, *George Washington, The Christian*, 197-198.

71 Freeman, *Washington: A Biography*, xxiv.

72 At a meeting at the City Tavern in Georgetown, when provisions for the Society of the Cincinnati were being formulated, Washington became first President-General. He expected that the Society of the Cincinnati be created to care for his troops, their wid-

ows and children. He insisted that the delegates to the Society 'strike out every word, sentence and clause which has a political tendency'. See Freeman, *Washington: A Biography*, 520.

73 See Aikman, *Rider with a Destiny*, 115-123.

74 Chief Justice John Marshall as quoted in Freeman, *Washington: A Biography*, xxiv.

75 Ibid., 100.

76 Catholicism has undergone many changes since the time of George Washington. Today's view of the hierarchy is far different from the political realities in place at the time of George Washington. The American political ideal of the Founders of the United States too has undergone metamorphoses. This generation hears the call to revive the ideal.

77 George Washington, Letter to Colonel Benedict Arnold, September 14, 1775.

78 Ibid.

79 Freeman, *Washington: A Biography*, 39.

80 Ibid., 41.

81 Ibid., 56.

82 Ibid., 585.

83 Schroeder, *Maxims of Washington*, 178.

84 George Washington letter to Samuel Langdon, September 28, 1789.

85 Alden, *George Washington*, 146.

[86] Ibid., 149.

[87] Quoting Forrest McDonald in Gregg and Spalding, *Patriot Sage*, 25, 26.

[88] Washington's letter to Secretary of State, July 29, 1795, as he was recalled to military duty. As quoted in Schroeder, *Maxims of Washington*, 142.

[89] Dickinson and Jefferson: Declaration of the Causes and Necessity of Taking Up Arms.

[90] In the Mount Vernon collection is a document in Washington's handwriting in which he carefully kept account of his out-of-pocket expenses, and specifically Martha Washington's traveling expenses to and from his quarters during the war years.

[91] Washington letter to Reverend Jonathan Boucher, Dec. 16, 1777.

[92] Ibid.

[93] Washington's letter to his wife: June 18, 1775.

[94] Washington had been heard to say of the British Parliament: "[T]hey have no more right to put their hands into my pocket, without my consent, than I have to put my hands into yours for money." As quoted in Bradford, *Founding Fathers*, 128.

[95] Washington's letter to Martha Washington, June 18, 1775.

[96] Ibid.

[97] Less faith-filled colonists of means, believing the cause of independence was lost, were forging personal

alliances in the salons of Philadelphia with British diplomats. Many less committed colonists would go to England to live.

98 See memorabilia at Valley Forge Museum, Valley Forge, PA.

99 The National Tribune, Volume 4, No. 12, December 1880.

100 Janice T. Connell, Angel Power (New York: Ballantine Books, 1995), 203-219.

101 *Woodstock Letters, Reflections*, Volume 13, 1884. Curtsey of Rev. Thomas King, S.J., Theology Department, Georgetown University, Washington, DC., Woodstock Letters: Volume 13, 1884, reveals the familial friendship between Bishop Carroll and General Washington.

102 Woodstock Letters, Reflections, Volume 13, 1884, p. 388. Courtesy of Rev. Thomas King, S. J. , Theology Department, Georgetown University, Washington, DC.

103 From the Basilica of the National Shrine of the Assumption of the Blessed Virgin Mary, Baltimore, MD. The author extends heartfelt thanks to Rosemary and Charles Carroll Carter for their graciousness in making available their family historical data concerning Archbishop John Carroll.

104 "The Old Testament theophanies of God in human form radiate from the ontological mystery of the Incarnation and the Theotokas in the New Testament. The Incarnation is the cause of creation and the source of all revelation. ...Without a human form, ...He could not be known....Because of the Mother of God, saints and angels were able to speak with God, 'mouth to mouth' [seeing Him] in a form and not in riddles." Num. 12: 8. As quoted in George S. Gabriel, *Mary The Untrodden Portal of God* (Ridgewood, NJ: Zephyr Publishing. 2000), 119. Courtesy of Rev. Victor Potopov, Pastor, St. John the Baptist Russian Orthodox Cathedral, Washington, DC.

[105] Gabriel, *Mary The Untrodden Portal of God*, 24.

[106] Ibid, quoting Patristic Father Saint Iranaeus.

[107] See Connell, *Meetings with Mary*. Op Cit.

[108] The National Tribune, Volume 4, No. 12, December 1880 obtained from the Library of Congress through the graciousness of The Honorable Margaret Mary Heckler.

[109] Reproduced ver batum from the original published journal preserved at the Library of Congress. Access to this document was obtained through the courtesy of the Hon. Margaret Heckler.

[110] Thomas O'Brien Hanley, *Charles Carroll of Carrollton: The Making of a Revolutionary Gentleman* (Chicago: Loyola University Press, 1982), 260.

[111] Morison and Commager, *The Growth of the American Republic*, 1:221.

[112] Ibid., 223.

[113] Ibid.

[114] George Washington's letter to Marquis de Lafayette, June 19, 1788, George Washington, Writings Vol. 29 p. 526 as quoted in Schroeder, *Maxims of Washington*, 51.

115 Jefferson's letter to John Adams, October 28, 1813.

116 Jefferson's letter to Dr. Benjamin Rush, September 23, 1800.

117 Alden, *George Washington*, 80.

118 Ibid., 79.

119 Joseph E. Fields, *Worthy Partner: The Papers of Martha Washington* (Westport, CT: Greenwood Press, 1994), ix.

120 Ibid.

121 Schroeder, *Maxims of Washington*, 166, Writings Vol. 30 p.289.

122 Morison and Commager, *The Growth of the American Republic*, 1:18.

123 Alden, *George Washington*, 81.

124 Genesis 12: 1-4.

125 Genesis 13: 4.

126 Alden, *George Washington*, 82.

127 Ibid.

128 Ibid., 83.

129 Ibid.

130 Ibid., 93.

131 Aikman, *Rider with a Destiny*, 144.

132 Letter to John Christian Ehler, Philadelphia, December 23, 1793.

133 Washington's letter to Henry Knox, Mount Vernon, April 1, 1789.

134 Letter of George Washington to Tobias Lear, 31 July, 1797.

135 Hanley, *Charles Carroll of Carrollton*, 150.

136 Ibid., 152.

137 Bradford, *Founding Fathers*, 125.

138 Washington, as quoted in Freeman, *Washington: A Biography*, 740.

139 Ibid., 745.

140 Johnson, *Washington, The Christian*, 231-232.

141 As quoted in Freeman, *Washington: A Biography*, 748.

142 Johnson, *Washington, The Christian*, 226-227, quoting Elizabeth Bryant Johnson, George Washington, *Day By Day*, 1894.

143 Roger Bruns, ed. *George Washington: World Leaders-Past and Present* (Broomall, PA: Chelsea House Publishers, 1987), 109.

144 Ibid., 110.

145 Dorothy Twohig, ed. *George Washington's Diaries. An Abridgment.* (Charlottesville and London: University Press of Virginia, 1999), 428-431.

146 Statement of Mother Theresa of Calcutta given personally to author.

147 Freeman, *Washington: A Biography*, 749.

148 Alden, *George Washington*, 303.

149 Douglas Southall Freeman. Washington. op. cit. p. 751.

150 *The soul of a righteous man is a Paradise in which God takes delight.* Proverbs 8:31.

151 Volume 20, 1893, p. 498, Answer to Queries of July, 1893, the following affidavit is recorded: " Father Neale, S.J. …baptized Washington on his death-bed. My authority was a Mrs. Darling, living in Baltimore. Her grandmother, Mrs. Mulineux, was first cousin to Washington. She stated to me and has, since, stated to others that such is the tradition in her family. Mrs. Darling is a convert [to Catholicism] and very friendly to Father Ardia and other fathers of this community. With the greatest respect In Christ Yours, P. Aloysius Jordan, Loyola, Baltimore, August 1, 1893." For further information, contact Rev. Thomas King, S.J., or Rev. Paul Chaufey, S. J., Georgetown University, Washington, DC. More documentation may be available in the archives of the Society of Jesus at Wernersville, MD. See also Twohig, *George Washington's Diaries*, 425.

152 Flexner, *Washington the Indispensable Man*, 399,400.

153 Freeman, *Washington: A Biography*, 752.

154 Ibid.

155 On April 12, 2003, immediately after the fall of Baghdad, Gerard Baker of the International Financial Times Limited said in his Comment and Analysis article entitled "The Land of the Free Enjoys the Thrill of Being a Force for Good:"

..."It is this self-faith as much as anything that
defines and differentiates Americans from most of
the rest of the world. ...Americans, almost alone in
the world, have a serios, unironic, uncynical, even
simplistic belief that their country is a force for
enduring good. They acknowledge it does not
always get it right, that at times its antics fall far
short of its highest ideals, but all but the most
hardened cynics really believe in America as a
force for freedom and prosperity and in the univer-
sality of these goals. This belief is born of the country's history, religion and culture....

"For most of the rest of the world, this ingenious
faith in the nation's unyielding will and power to
produce beneficial outcomes for everybody is
almost non-existant.... But you can hardly blame
Americans...for thinking that they sit on the right
side of history. And you surely cannot help but
marvel at the fact that they are almost alone in
seeing themselves that way."

156 George Washington's Thanksgiving Proclamation,
October 3, 1789. As quoted in Schroeder, *Maxims of
Washington*, 172.

Illustration Credits

1 Photograph No. NWDNS-148-GW-46; **"Washington, George, the Virginia Colonel,"** 1772; George Washington Bicentennial Commission, Record Group 148; National Archives at College Park, College Park, MD.

2 "Life of George Washington--The Citizen;" Junius Brutus Stears, artist; Library of Congress, Prints and Photography Division [LC-USZ62-3914].

3 **"Mount Vernon in Virginia;"** Francis Jukes, engraver; Library of Congress, Prints and Photography Division [LC-USZ62-1237].

4 Photograph No. NWDNS-148-GW-1141; **"Reading of the Declaration of Independence from the East balcony of the Old State House, Boston, Massachusetts July 18, 1776,"** Copy of artwork, 1931-1932; George Washington Bicentennial Commission, Record Group 148; National Archives at College Park, College Park, MD.

5   Photograph   No.   NWDNS-148-GW-571; **"Washington Taking Command of the American Army, at Cambridge, Massachusetts July 3rd, 1775,"** Copy of Lithograph by Currier & Ives, 1876; George Washington Bicentennial Commission, Record Group 148; National Archives at College Park, College Park, MD.

6   Photograph   No.   NWDNS-148-GW-580; **"Washington at the Battle of Trenton. Decemeber 1776,"** Copy of engraving by Illman Brothers after E. L. Henry, circa 1870; George Washington Bicentennial Commission, Record Group 148; National Archives at College Park, College Park, MD.

7   Photograph No. NWDNS-148-GW-189; **"Valley Forge-Washington & Lafayette. Winter 1777-78,"** Copy of engraving by H.B. Hall after Alonzo Chappel, 1931-1932; George Washington Bicentennial Commission, Record Group 148; National Archives at College Park, College Park, MD.

8   Photograph No. NWDNS-148-GW-201; **"The Prayer at Valley Forge. General George Washington, winter 1777-78."** Copy of engraving by John C. McRae after Henry Brueckner, published 1866; George Washington Bicentennial Commission, Record Group 148; National Archives at College Park, College Park, MD.

Selected Bibliography

Aikman, Lonnelle. *Rider with A Destiny: George Washington*. McLean, VA: Link Press Publishers, 1983.

Alden, John R. *George Washington: A Biography*. Baton Rouge, LA: Louisiana State University Press, 1981.

Bradford, M.E. *Founding Fathers: Brief Lives of the Framers of the United States Constitution*. 2nd ed. Lawrence, KS: University Press of Kansas, 1994.

Bruns, Roger, ed. *George Washington (World Leaders-Past and Present)*. Broomall, PA: Chelsea House Publishers, 1987.

Burk, Herbert W. *Washington's Prayers*. Norristown, PA: Published for the Benefit of the Washington Memorial Chapel, 1907.

Clark, Harrison. *All Cloudless Glory: The Life of George Washington*. 2 vols. Washington, DC: Regnery Publications, Inc., 1995.

Ellis, Joseph J. *Founding Brothers: The Revolutionary Generation*. New York: Alfred A. Knopf, 2000.

Ferling, John. *Setting the World Ablaze: Washington, Adams, Jefferson, and the American Revolution*. New York: Oxford University Press, 2000.

Fields, Joseph E. *Worthy Partner: The Papers of Martha Washington*. Westport, CT: Greenwood Press, 1994.

Flexner, James T. *Washington The Indispensable Man*. Boston: Little, Brown & Company, 1969.

Freeman, Douglas S. *Washington: A Biography*. With an introduction by Michael Kammen, and afterword by Dumas Malone. An Abridgment by Richard Harwell. New York: Touchstone, 1968.

Gregg, Gary L., and Matthew Spalding, eds. *Patriot Sage: George Washington and the American Political Tradition*. Wilmington, DE: ISI Books, 1999.

Hanley, Thomas O'Brien. *Charles Carroll of Carrollton: The Making of a Revolutionary Gentleman.* Chicago: Loyola University Press, 1982.

Hawke, David F. *Everyday Life in Early America.* New York: Harper & Row, 1988.

Higginbotham, Don. *The War of American Independence: Military Attitudes, Policies, and Practice, 1763-1789.* New York: Macmillan, 1971.

Johnson, Gerald W. *Mount Vernon: The Story of a Shrine.* Mount Vernon, VA: Mount Vernon Ladies Association, 1991.

Johnson, William J. *George Washington, The Christian.* Arlington, TX: Christian Liberty Press, 1919.

Langguth, A.J. *Patriots: The Men Who Started the American Revolution.* New York: Simon & Schuster, 1988.

Lucas, Stephen E., ed. *The Quotable George Washington.* Madison, WI: Madison House Publishers, Inc. 1999.

McCullough, David. *John Adams*. NY: Simon & Schuster, 2001.

McDonald, Forest. *The Presidency of George Washington*. Lawrence, KS: University Press of Kansas, 1974.

Morison, Samuel E., Henry Steele Commager, and William Leuchtenburg, eds. *A Concise History of the American Republic*. New York: Oxford University Press, 1958.

Morison, Samuel E., and Henry Steele Commager. *The Growth of the American Republic*. 2 vols. New York: Oxford University Press, 1958.

Needleman, Jacob. *The American Soul: Rediscovering the Wisdom of the Founders*. New York: Jeremy P. Tarcher/Putnam, 2002.

Novak, Michael. *On Two Wings: Humble Faith and Common Sense at the American Founding*. San Francisco, CA: Encounter Books, 2002.

Phillips, John T., ed. *George Washington's Rules of Civility*. Leesburg, VA: Goose Creek Productions, 2000.

Schroeder, John F., ed. *Maxims of Washington, Political, Social, Moral, and Religious*. With an introduction by Gerald R. Ford. Mount Vernon, VA: Mount Vernon Ladies Association, 1989.

Sharp, James R. *American Politics in the Early Republic: The New Nation in Crisis*. New Haven, CT: Yale University Press, 1993.

Shy, John W. *A People Numerous and Armed: Reflections on the Military Struggle for American Independence*. Ann Arbor, MI: University of Michigan Press, 1990.

Tuchman, Barbara W. *The First Salute*. New York: Knopf, 1988.

Twohig, Dorothy, ed. *George Washington's Diaries*. Charlottesville, VA and London: University Press of Virginia, 1999.

Ward, Christopher. *The War of the Revolution.* 11 vols. New York: Macmillan, 1952.

Wills, Garry. *Cincinnatus: George Washington and the Enlightenment.* Garden City, NY: Doubleday, 1984.